APPLES, APPLES, EVERYWHERE

FAVORITE RECIPES FROM AMERICA'S ORCHARDS

Lee Jackson

Illustrations by Terri Wilson and Others

Images Unlimited Publishing
P. O. Box 305
Maryville, Missouri
64468

Published by:

Images Unlimited Publishing
P.O. Box 305
Maryville, Missouri 64468
(816) 582-4279
(800) 356-9315

First Edition—1996

10 9 8 7 6 5 4 3 2

Also by Lee Jackson:
Nutrition/Exercise Program   *manual and cassette*
From the Apple Orchard - Recipes for Apple Lovers
Careers in Focus: Family and Consumer Sciences

Printed and bound in the United States of America.

Library of Congress Catalog Card Number 95-79981

ISBN 0-930643-11-3   Softcover

CONTENTS

Introduction   iv

Beverages   1
Breads   7
    Pancakes   10
    Coffee Cakes   14
    Muffins   21
    Loaf Breads   28
Salads   41
Main Dishes   61
Accompaniments   69
Cookies   87
Cakes   103
    Toppings for Cakes   140
Pies and Pastry   141
Desserts   177
Jams, Preserves, Etc.   231
Special Treats   239
Orchard Directory   243
Recipe Index   249

Introduction

Now you can read about some of the great orchards of this country as well as many small "Mom and Pop" orchards, all having the same zeal for growing the best, most flavorful apples in the world. Apples have a long and interesting history. Records indicate that as long as 20 centuries ago man understood the art of budding and grafting fruit trees. Apple orchards were planted in China and Egypt and all over Europe. The settlers brought with them apple seeds and planted their first apple crops in the New World. There are now hundreds of apple varieties in the United States and several thousand in the world.

On the following pages you will follow a bit of apple history in America. Many of the orchards you will read about go back 4 or 5 generations. The lives of countless families have revolved around the eternal hope for that "perfect" crop. Each year is the same, yet different.

This book is dedicated to the orchard growers and apple enthusiasts who so graciously shared their recipes, history, and their love of the land. It is my hope that others will appreciate and protect this land, our legacy, and may its fruit continue to bless our tables and satisfy body and soul.

To the reader, it is hoped that this cookbook will be a source of many new ideas for preparing apples. By themselves, apples are tasty and good nutritionally. Being relatively low in calories, an average apple contains about 80 calories. They provide quick energy because of their natural sugar content. Apples vary in sweetness, therefore, sugar may be decreased in many recipes.

To decrease the amount of sugar in recipes, try reducing the amount by one-quarter to one-third in baked goods and desserts. This works best in quick breads, cookies, and desserts. It may be less desirable for some cakes. An increase in the amount of cinnamon or vanilla in a recipe tends to enhance the impression of sweetness.

Applesauce can be used to replace fat in many recipes. Use equal amounts of applesauce to fat. For example, instead of using 1/2 cup butter or margarine, use 1/2 cup unsweetened applesauce, or for a moderate amount of fat, use 1/4 cup butter and 1/4 cup unsweetened applesauce. In many recipes, the amount of fat can be decreased by one-fourth to one-third. These suggestions can be applied to most foods except those that are essential to prevent spoilage, such as in jams and jellies or are needed to ensure a standard quality product, such as in yeast breads, cakes, and pie crusts.

BEVERAGES

Dunn's Cider Mill

Belton, Missouri

Cider sipping and scarecrow contests are some of the special events held at Dunn's Cider Mill each fall. Contestants are challenged to sip a measured amount of cider through a straw as fast as they can. The quickest in each age category wins. The scarecrow contest draws entries from individuals, families, schools, scout troops, youth groups, hospitals, nursing homes, and businesses. The scarecrows are on public display until Halloween and draw several thousand viewers.

Dunn's Cider Mill produces natural cider straight from the press, with no additives whatsoever. Cider donuts are made at the mill every day. Other products for sale besides apples include honey, sorghum, apple and peach butter, cashews, pumpkins, ice cream, and gift items. The mill is open daily from mid-September through mid-December.

HOT SPICED CIDER

Start with cider that has not been treated with preservatives. Read the fine print on the label.

Use a ceramic, Pyrex™, or stainless steel container for heating. Avoid aluminum as it imparts a metallic flavor.

Combine the following ingredients in the container:
1/2 gallon cider
8-inch stick cinnamon
12 whole cloves
4 allspice berries (or 1/4 teaspoon powdered allspice)

Cover and bring to a near boil. Turn to the lowest heat setting and let steep one half hour.

"The longer the cider remains heated the stronger the spice taste becomes."

Jon Chapin Dunn
Dunn's Cider Mill
Belton, Missouri

Bob's Bluebird Orchard and Craft Barn

Webster, Minnesota

Bob's Bluebird Orchard is nestled in the rolling green hills that border the Minnesota River Valley. This is a small, family owned operation run by Bob and Linda Leis and their two daughters, Laura and Andrea. Bob began planting apple trees in 1983, and now they have 27 varieties of apples, including the new Minnesota introduction, *Honey Crisp*, on approximately 1,000 trees. Apples are sold at their farm, as well as at the St. Paul Farmers' Market twice a week during apple season.

In addition to growing apples, the Leis family harbor an abiding interest in encouraging and preserving the natural environment — especially bird life. They love seeing nesting bluebirds in and near the orchard, thus the orchard name, "Bob's Bluebird Orchard."

OLD-FASHIONED APPLE PUNCH

2 quarts apple juice
3 cinnamon sticks
12 whole cloves
1 cup orange juice
28 ounces 7-Up™
1 *Cortland* apple, thinly sliced

Simmer 1 quart apple juice with spices for 10 minutes. Refrigerate
several hours or overnight to develop full spice flavor. Discard
cinnamon and cloves. Combine mixture and remaining chilled apple
and orange juice in large punch bowl. Slowly pour in chilled 7-Up ™.
Garnish with thin apple slices. Makes 26 cups.

Bob and Linda Leis
Bob's Bluebird Orchard
Webster, Minnesota

The Ridge Orchards
Bourbon, Missouri

Cider Rain
by Leona Heitsch

The record drought slides out
this morning
...it's mid-September
and today's unforgiving force
up from the Gulf
strikes an end to summer's
stubborn scorch.

This old spent hurricane
greets the south wall of the house
and slashes rain full in its' eyes.

Past the point of meeting
of the pane and driving rain
a strange late greening
in this autumn-tinged world.

The orchard sways in a dawn moire,
the dancing gold delicious spheres
that gild the laden branches
drinking in
the storm-borne draught.

BREADS

Rum River Orchard
Milaca, Minnesota

As Jan Anderson said about their apple growing experience, "It's hard to makes one's dreams brief." Here are excerpts from her letter:
"No money, no know-how, a bit naïve, access to land, and a wild dream — that's how it all started.

My favorite orchard just outside the metro area had gotten so commercial, so large. Parking was now handled by a dozen orange flag-waving students and you felt as if you were at the state fair, lost in the masses of people. The idea began to take shape—a cozy orchard bordered by the woods, surrounded by natural brush and habitat.

Armed with library books, I called the University Extension Service to find out what apples were best for my apple orchard up north. They strongly suggested I get land further south. I explained this land was free. It was part of my father-in-law's farm. They then suggested I plant strawberries if I wanted to grow and sell fruit. I could not be swayed. After all, we built our dome home with no prior building experience, no carpenter knowledge, and no idea what a major challenge building was going to be! I felt we could do anything and everything!

In 1982, holes were dug and ten apple trees were planted. Visions of blooming apple trees surrounding our dome danced in my head. That winter, nine of the ten apple trees were mowed down by my brother-in-law and his friends riding snow mobiles.

Not to be discouraged, more holes were dug. Seventy trees were planted. I learned over the next few years about trees and dreams. Did I ever learn! The land needed to be cleared. The "natural habitat" I envisioned could not remain under trees, or even near where they were planted, but could only surround the orchard at the edges. More trees died, and a lot more trees were planted.

These trees were getting to be a lot of work and they weren't even in production yet. But I continued to dream about the future.

People would ask "What are you going to do with all those apples if they ever do produce?" They laughed when I boldly answered, "I'll sell them!"

I used to be known as the "igloo lady" (our dome home), now I was "the lady with the fruitless orchard!" However, I still kept working in that orchard, and finally, three apples appeared! The deer ate two of them.

The following winter of 1985, the dreams stopped. I went blind in one eye — the diagnosis was swift and brutal. I had Multiple Sclerosis (M.S.) and was told, "By the way, that difficulty you have had with your legs the last five years, well, that's M.S., too."

My vision eventually came back, but emotionally and physically I was still staggering. That summer everyone was polite. No one asked what I was going to do with the apples now starting to appear on close to a hundred trees.

The deer appeared to enjoy them and the rest we cooked or gave away. I still enjoyed riding the mower in the orchard, but there was no dreaming. The following year, I started to hear gentle suggestions that we let the orchard go wild or have my father-in-law bulldoze it down. Wouldn't you know, my father-in-law has his own bulldozer!

Somehow, the dreams started to come back. After all, my legs have been bad for years and I still was able to maneuver my environment to accommodate myself. I still continued to have the loving support of my husband, Gene, a very hard worker.

After attending an apple conference and some apple growers monthly meetings, Gene and I were encouraged to open for business. Labor day week-end, 1989, we put out a few picnic tables to hold the apples, a sign out on the highway, and, with the help of our seven-year-old nephew, Jared, we were open for business.

Now, several years later, we have three orchards "hidden" in our natural habitat, an apple shed, tables for picnics, and one very special out-doors apple checker-board, a favorite among children and their parents.

In October, the pumpkin patch comes alive with our display of scarecrows and the laughter of children selecting their pumpkins. Gourds, pumpkins, and dry flowers are for sale along with our apples, cider, jellies and crafts. People still describe our place as "cozy, tucked into the woods and beautiful." And I am now called 'the Apple Lady'!"

GENE'S OVEN PANCAKES

3 eggs
2 or 3 apples, peeled and cut in slices
3/4 cup flour
3/4 cup milk
1 teaspoon vanilla
Dash of cinnamon
1/2 stick butter or margarine

Heat oven to 425° F. Using a non-stick oven proof 9-10 inch frying pan, melt butter in pan in oven. In blender, blend 3 eggs. Add flour and milk alternately while eggs are blending. Add vanilla; blend 1 minute. Pour into heated pan with melted butter. Add apple slices. Sprinkle top of mixture with cinnamon to taste. Bake at 425° F. for 20 minutes. When done, turn pan upside down onto plate. Serve with syrup.

"Pancake puffs up and then deflates, so don't panic."

Jan and Gene Anderson
Rum River Orchard
Milaca, Minnesota

Carlson's Orchard
Winsted, Minnesota

Carlson's Orchard and Farm Bakery is situated on 200 acres of what was once a Dakota Nation encampment. The Orchard property borders the east shore of an old lake, Butternut Lake, site of this encampment. One day in 1979 while picking rocks from the field prior to planting, Joe Carlson discovered a stone ax head, the first of 100 Native American artifacts.

Apples were considered an alternative farming method in 1982 while Joe Carlson lived in Oregon and traveled the Northwest as a salesman. The idea of growing apples was brought to the Minnesota family farm, and in 1985, the first of 3500 apple trees were planted, following practices common in Northwest apple orchards.

Carlson's Orchard produces 12 varieties of apples, primarily Minnesota developed varieties. These include *Haralson, Honeygold, State Fair, Keepsake, Honeycrisp*, and *Fireside*. The varieties allow for an early start on the season, a late ending, and appeal to everyone in between. All apples are hand picked and graded through the orchard's sorting line.

In 1994 the Carlsons remodeled and relocated their apple selling business to the original barn, which was an early prefab, erected in 1933 in just 2 days. A state-approved full service bakery and a complete cider room were installed, along with the enlargement of their cooler. Fresh, hot pie and ice cream are served in their restaurant area.

APPLE PUFF PANCAKE

Layered raisins and apples form the foundation for this European-style brunch offering. It's baked in a pie pan, but without the traditional pastry crust. Prepared in advance, it can be warmed up at serving time. A smooth custard sauce adds extra appeal.

2 tablespoons butter
2 cups peeled, sliced apples (about 2 medium)
1/2 cup golden raisins
2 eggs
3/4 cup water
3/4 cup flour
1/4 cup non-fat dry milk
2 tablespoons sugar

Melt butter in 9 inch pie plate in a 425° F. oven. Layer half of apples, then raisins, then remaining apples in melted butter. Cover with foil. Return to oven and bake 10 minutes. Beat eggs with wire whisk in medium bowl. Add water, flour, dry non-fat milk and sugar; beat just until blended. Pour over sizzling hot apple mixture. Bake uncovered in 425° F. oven for 15 to 20 minutes or until deep golden and puffed. Cut into wedges and serve warm with *Cinnamon Custard Sauce*. Yields 6 to 8 servings.

Cinnamon Custard Sauce
1/2 cup non-fat dry milk
1/4 cup sugar
4 teaspoons cornstarch
1/2 teaspoon cinnamon
1/8 teaspoon salt
1 cup water
1 well-beaten egg yolk
1/2 teaspoon vanilla

Combine non-fat milk, sugar, cornstarch, cinnamon, and salt in small saucepan. Gradually stir in water. Cook over medium-low heat, stirring constantly, until mixture comes to a full boil. Remove from heat. Beat small amount of hot mixture into egg yolk. Return saucepan to heat. Stir egg mixture back into mixture in saucepan. Cook, stirring constantly, until mixture just comes to a boil and thickens. Remove from heat. Stir in vanilla. Yields: 1 1/3 cups.

Colleen Carlson
Carlsons Orchard and Farm Bakery
Winsted, Minnesota

Honey Hill Orchard
Waterman, Illinois

Honey Hill Orchard is located 8 miles south of DeKalb, Illinois and is owned by Steve and Kathy Bock. Even though they are in a very rural area, they are only 30 minutes from the Chicago suburbs.

The Bocks strive to keep a down-home country atmosphere. An old farm barn was converted into the Apple Sales Barn, complete with a "Feeding Trough", where apple products are sold.

QUICK APPLE NUT COFFEE CAKE

1 package refrigerated buttermilk biscuits
3 tablespoons melted butter or margarine
2 large cooking apples, peeled, cored, and sliced
1/4 cup sugar
1/2 teaspoon cinnamon
1/4 cup chopped pecans

Dip biscuits in melted butter or margarine. Place in 9 inch round baking pan. Arrange apple slices on top of biscuits. Mix cinnamon and sugar. Sprinkle over apples. Sprinkle pecans over top. Drizzle with remaining butter. Bake at 350° F. for 30 minutes. Serve warm.

Steve and Kathy Bock
Honey Hill Orchard
Waterman, Illinois

Soergel Orchards
Wexford, Pennsylvania

The present Soergel Orchard was started as a farm in 1850 by John Conrad Soergel, a German immigrant. At that time the farm produce (mostly apples) was all sold in the wholesale market in Pittsburgh, Pennsylvania, located about thirteen miles south of the farm. The fifth generation is now working on the farm.

In 1960, a hard freeze left only a few apples on the trees. From a small retail market started at that time, their orchard business has continued to grow and flourish.

RAISIN HARVEST COFFEE CAKE

1 1/2 cups sifted flour
3 3/4 teaspoons baking powder
1/2 teaspoon salt
3/4 cup sugar
3/4 cup butter
2 cups peeled cooking apples, chopped fine
1 1/2 cups dark seedless raisins
2 large eggs
1 tablespoon milk
Sugar for topping

In mixing bowl, re-sift flour with baking powder, salt, and sugar. Add butter and mix until mixture is like fine bread crumbs. Stir in apples and raisins and add well-beaten eggs and milk. Beat thoroughly. Batter will be stiff. Spread in a well-greased 9 inch square pan . Sprinkle generously with sugar. Bake at 350° F. for 55-60 minutes. Allow to cool slightly before cutting. Serve warm.

Lillian "Toots" Berkshire
Soergel Orchards
Wexford, Pennsylvania

Ski-Hi Fruit Farm
Baraboo, Wisconsin

Situated on the ancient Devil's Lake bluff 1250 feet above sea level, Ski-Hi Fruit Farm is located five miles south of Baraboo, Wisconsin. The city of Baraboo is the home of the famous Ringling Bros. Circus, the Circus World Museum, and the beautiful playhouse, the Al Ringling Theatre.

In 1907, A. K. Bassett bought land on which Ski-Hi Fruit Farm now stands to fulfill his dream of raising apples and owning an apple orchard. He purchased the property from the Weidenkopf family, who received it as a grant from the U.S. government in 1857. A log cabin had been built on the property in 1863 and the land had already been cleared. Because the land was very rocky and the soil was heavy, clay loam, it was unsuitable for farm crops, but adaptable for apples. Mr. Bassett thus fulfilled his lifelong dream of raising apples.

The original log cabin located on the homestead forty has since been restored. It is furnished with many family antiques and can be seen upon request.

APPLE COFFEE CAKE

1 package (9-oz.) yellow cake mix
1 package (3 3/4 oz.) vanilla instant pudding mix
2 eggs
1/2 cup sour cream
1/4 cup melted butter

Combine above ingredients and beat five minutes.

Peel and thinly slice 2 medium apples.

Combine:
1/4 cup chopped nut meats
1/2 cup sugar
1 teaspoon cinnamon

Pour half the batter into greased 7 x 11 inch pan. Arrange apple
slices over batter. Sprinkle half nut mixture over slices. Spread
remainder batter over slices. Sprinkle nut mixture over top. Bake at
350° F. oven for 40 minutes. Serves 12.

Olga Marie Bassett
Ski-Hi Fruit Farm
Baraboo, Wisconsin

Ski-Hi Fruit Farm

"IN THE HEART OF THE HILLS"

Coon Creek Orchard
Armada, Michigan

Coon Creek Orchard is located in Armada, Michigan, which is in the southeastern part of the state, north of Detroit. The orchard was established in the mid 1970's by the Sattler family and purchased by Terence and Delores Lembke Brown in 1991.

The fruit crop consists of many varieties of apples, sweet and sour cherries, peaches, plums, pears, apricots, nectarines, strawberries, and raspberries. They offer customers a country atmosphere in a natural farm/orchard surrounding. All the crops can be picked by the customer and/or purchased from the farm market store or at various local farm markets.

Coon Creek's annual apple festival is held the third weekend in September. This includes live entertainment, refreshments, hay rides, pony rides, and many other activities. The orchard's country store offers a large variety of jams, jellies, apple butters, honeys, fruits, caramel apples, donuts, cider, coffee, pies and country crafts.

SOUR CREAM APPLE COFFEE CAKE

Coffee Cake Mixture
3 cups flour
2 teaspoons baking powder
1/2 teaspoon salt
1/2 teaspoon ground cinnamon
1/2 cup butter
1 1/2 cups sugar
3 eggs
1 1/2 cups sour cream
1 cup diced apple
1 teaspoon vanilla extract

Crumb Mixture
1/2 cup flour
1/2 cup sugar
1/4 cup butter
1/2 teaspoon cinnamon
1 cup chopped nuts

Combine all ingredients for the crumb mixture in a bowl. Mix until mixture resembles coarse crumbs — set aside.

For the coffee cake, combine flour, baking powder, salt, and cinnamon; set aside. Cream butter with sugar. Add eggs, sour cream, apple, and vanilla. Gradually stir in flour mixture. Beat at medium speed of mixer for approximately two minutes. Spoon about 2 cups of the batter into a well-greased twelve-cup fluted tube pan. Sprinkle with half of the reserved crumb mixture. Spoon another 2 cups of batter, spreading it to cover crumbs. Repeat layers with remaining crumb mixture and batter. Bake at 350° F. for 55 to 60 minutes. Sprinkle with confectioners' sugar just before serving. Makes 16 servings.

Delores Brown
Coon Creek Orchard
Armada, Michigan

Fleming Orchards
Gays Mills, Wisconsin

James Fleming is an apple grower who established Fleming Orchards in 1937. The original orchard of 20 acres was set by his father prior to World War II, in hopes that James would have a business when he returned from service. More acreage was set in the 1950's. The original orchard has been replaced and each year trees are removed and replaced with some new varieties. James Jr. has now joined the family tradition.

A large collection of antique carriages greets visitors to the Fleming Orchards. Squash, pumpkins, and gourds, as well as jams, cider, maple syrup, and honey are sold at the retail sales room. Their products are sold wholesale as well as retail.

APPLE STREUSEL MUFFINS

2 cups flour
1/2 cup sugar
1 tablespoon baking powder
1 teaspoon salt
1/2 cup butter (1 stick)
2 cups chopped apples (cored but unpeeled)
1 egg
2/3 cup milk

Preheat oven to 425° F. Grease muffin tin. Sift flour, sugar, baking powder, and salt into a large bowl. Cut in butter with fork or pastry blender until mixture is crumbly. Set aside 1/2 cup mixture for topping. Stir apples into remaining flour mixture. Beat egg and milk together; pour over apple mixture. Stir lightly only until evenly moist. Spoon into prepared muffin cups. Sprinkle topping over batter.

Topping
1/4 cup chopped walnuts
2 tablespoons sugar
1/2 teaspoon cinnamon

Stir nuts, sugar, and cinnamon into 1/2 cup reserved flour mixture. Bake in 425° F. oven for 16-20 minutes or until golden brown. Yield: 12 large muffins

Ruth M. Fleming
Fleming Orchards
Gays Mills, Wisconsin

Stephenson's Apple Tree Inn
Kansas City, Missouri

APPLE TREE INN

The Apple Tree Inn carries the famous entrées of Stephenson's restaurants. Apple fritters continue to be the favorite of all the guests. Hickory smoked meats are another Stephenson specialty.

The antique displays and country store present a unique touch to this famous eating establishment, located 8 miles south of Kansas City International Airport. Banquet rooms and an outdoor patio add to the comfort and convenience of their customers at The Apple Tree Inn.

FRESH APPLE MUFFINS

1 egg
1 cup milk
1/4 cup melted shortening
2/3 cup sugar
1/2 teaspoon salt
1/4 teaspoon cinnamon
1 teaspoon lemon juice
1/4 teaspoon vanilla
2 cups unsifted flour
3 teaspoons baking powder
1 cup unpeeled chopped apples

Beat egg. Stir in milk, shortening, sugar, salt, cinnamon, lemon juice, and vanilla. Sift together flour and baking powder. Stir into milk mixture until blended. Do not overmix. Fold in apples. Spoon into greased muffin cups 2/3 full. Bake 450° F. degree about 20 minutes or until brown.
Makes: twelve 3" muffins

Steve Stephenson
Stephenson's Apple Tree Inn
Kansas City, Missouri

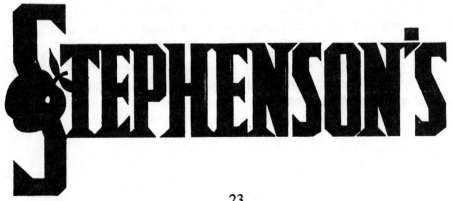

Ski-Hi Fruit Farm
Baraboo, Wisconsin

Ski-Hi Fruit Farm has been farmed continuously by the Bassett family for over eighty-seven years. In 1908, Mr. Bassett married a local girl, Emma Martin, and moved into the original log cabin. To them were born three children, Josephine, Jessie, and Arthur, Jr.

With the passing of A. K. Bassett, Sr., in 1961, Arthur, Jr. and his wife, Olga, continued to propagate the apples and carry on the orchard tradition, along with their son, Philip Arthur and daughter, Betty Marie. Arthur K., Jr. passed away December 14, 1983, having served his profession well. Olga, and her daughter, Betty Marie Bassett Thiessen, business manager, continue the family enterprise. Along with children and grandchildren, four generations have now been involved in this operation.

APPLE MUFFINS

1 1/2 cups flour
2 teaspoons baking powder
1/2 teaspoon salt
1/4 teaspoon nutmeg
1/2 cup sugar
1/3 cup shortening
1 egg
1/3 cup milk
1 1/2 cups pared, shredded apples

Sift together flour, baking powder, salt, and nutmeg and set aside. In mixing bowl, cream sugar and shortening. Add egg and beat well. Blend in milk alternately with dry ingredients. Stir in shredded apples. Fill well-greased muffin tins 2/3 full. Bake at 350° F. for 20 to 25 minutes until golden brown.

Dip tops in 1/4 cup melted butter and then in a mixture of 1/2 cup sugar and 1/4 teaspoon cinnamon. Serve hot. Muffins freeze well. Yield: 1 dozen.

Olga Marie Bassett
Ski-Hi Fruit Farm
Baraboo, Wisconsin

Ski-Hi Fruit Farm

"IN THE HEART OF THE HILLS"

The Ridge Orchards
Bourbon, Missouri

In the fall of 1973, Charles and Leona Heitsch purchased an abandoned ridge farm and began setting out apple trees the following spring. Leona came from an orchard background in Oakland County, Michigan. Her father, Russell Mason, managed a large orchard that was capable of producing 17,000 bushels per year. This was quite in contrast to the Heitschs' scaled down experimental enterprise in Missouri.

The Heitschs were pleased to be informed by a neighbor that in years past, their droughty, rocky ridgetop had been an orchard site, established by Elijah Greenlee, an early Stark Tree Agent. He sold apples from a horse-cart in the surrounding territory, including Bourbon, Sullivan, and Richwoods, Missouri. It was said that passersby were delighted to share fresh fruit and cider with him. Only one apple tree survived from Mr. Greenlee's orchard. This was identified by fellow members of North American Fruit Explorers (NAFEX) as a *Beitingheimer,* an old German variety. The fact that it survived testifies to its resistance to drought, disease, and insects. Scions of this tree and of several other early varieties, and newer ones, too, have been grafted to rootstocks, and are currently bearing.

Some of the scions from the Michigan home orchard grafted onto rootstocks included an almost forgotten apple, *Steele's Red*, which is an excellent eating apple and superb keeper.

A.B.C. MUFFINS
(Apple - Buckwheat - Cinnamon)

1 cup unbleached white flour
1 cup buckwheat flour
2 teaspoons baking powder
2 teaspoons cinnamon
1/2 cup honey
1 egg
1 cup cider (or milk)
1 cup finely chopped apple

Mix together dry ingredients. Add honey, egg, and cider or milk. Mix only until dry ingredients are moistened. Gently fold in apples. Spoon into well-greased muffin pans. Bake at 350° F. for 15-23 minutes. Makes 1 dozen muffins.

Leona Heitsch
The Ridge Orchards
Bourbon, Missouri

Rum River Orchard
Milaca, Minnesota

Nestled in the north lake country of Minnesota you will find the orchard of Gene and Jan Anderson. May they continue to nourish and live their dream!

APPLE BREAD

1/2 cup shortening
1 cup sugar
2 eggs
1/2 teaspoon vanilla
1 1/2 tablespoons milk
2 cups flour
1/2 teaspoon salt
1 teaspoon baking soda
2 teaspoons baking powder
1 1/2 cups chopped apples
2 tablespoons brown sugar
1 teaspoon nutmeg
2 1/2 tablespoons sugar
1 teaspoon cinnamon

Cream shortening and sugar. Beat in eggs, vanilla, and milk. Sift together flour, salt, baking soda, and baking powder. Stir into creamed mixture. Stir in chopped apples. Spoon 1/2 of batter into greased 9 x 5 inch loaf pan. Combine brown sugar, nutmeg, 2 1/2 tablespoons sugar, and cinnamon. Spoon 1/2 of brown sugar mixture over the batter. Spoon on the remaining batter and sprinkle remaining sugar mixture over the top. Bake in 350° F. oven about 1 hour or until done. Makes one loaf.

Jan Anderson
Rum River Orchard
Milaca, Minnesota

APPLE-RAISIN LOAVES

3 eggs
1 1/2 cups vegetable oil
2 cups chopped, unpared apples
1 1/2 cups sugar
1 teaspoon vanilla
3 1/3 cups flour
2 teaspoons baking soda
1 teaspoon baking powder
1 teaspoon salt
1 teaspoon cinnamon
1 teaspoon cloves
2/3 cup chopped nuts
2/3 cup raisins

Heat oven to 350° F. Grease and flour 2 loaf pans, 9 x 5 x 3 inches. Beat eggs, oil, apples, sugar, and vanilla on low speed of mixer for 1 minute, scraping bowl occasionally. Add flour, baking soda, baking powder, salt, cinnamon, and cloves. Beat on low speed, scraping bowl occasionally, until moistened, about 15 seconds. Beat on medium speed 45 seconds. Stir in nuts and raisins. Spread in pans. Bake at 350° F. for 55-60 minutes or until wooden pick inserted in center comes out clean. Cool 10 minutes; remove from pans. Cool completely before slicing.

Nina Layner
Layner Orchards
Little Hocking, Ohio

29

The Apple Barn at Hope Orchards

Hope, Maine

Hope Orchards, originally planted in 1935, probably were one of the first "pick your own" orchards in the state of Maine. Karl and Linda Drechsler purchased the farm in 1982 and have been replanting the orchard to dwarf and semi-dwarf apple trees, adding pears and a few peaches. The orchard is on 60 acres of land and is operated with harvest help for picking, packing, and selling. Their area has a few small orchards, hundreds of acres of wild low bush blueberries, and some dairy farms. They are 6 miles from the ocean and the area is a big tourist destination

Karl is a fourth generation apple grower. "And", says Linda, "Perhaps, one day, our son, Derek, now only two, will also grow apples."

APPLE/NUT/CHEESE BREAD

1/2 cup butter
3/4 cup sugar
2 eggs
1 3/4 cups flour
1 teaspoon baking powder
1/2 teaspoon baking soda
1/2 teaspoon salt
1/4 teaspoon ginger
1 cup grated apples
(*McIntosh* or *Cortland*)
1/2 cup grated cheddar cheese
1/3 cup chopped nuts

Grease 8 x 5 x 3 inch loaf pan. Cream butter, adding sugar a little at a time. Add eggs, beating after each. Combine flour, baking powder, baking soda, salt, and ginger. Add to first mixture, alternating with the apples. Stir in the cheese and nuts. Spoon into greased pan. Bake in preheated 350° F. oven about 1 hour. Cool well before cutting. Yield: 10 slices.

Linda and Karl Drechsler
The Apple Barn at Hope Orchards
Hope, Maine

The Apple Works
Trafalgar, Indiana

Just south of Indianapolis in south central Indiana, you'll find The Apple Works Orchard checkering the gently rolling hillsides of lower Johnson county. The glacier stopped there, sculpting the hills and leaving rich clay-loam and minerals on which their crops thrive.

Besides apples, Rick and Sarah Brown, along with their daughters Alison and Maggie, grow their own sweet corn, pumpkins and gourds, strawberries, blackberries, and pears. They enjoy the bounty of their part of Indiana and invite others to come and visit them at their orchard.

APPLE BREAD

1 cup sugar
1/2 cup shortening
2 eggs
1 teaspoon vanilla
2 cups flour
1 teaspoon baking powder
1 teaspoon baking soda
1/2 teaspoon salt
2 cups apples, pared and chopped
(about 4 medium)
1/2 cup chopped nuts
1 tablespoon sugar
1/4 teaspoon cinnamon

Preheat oven to 350° F. Grease and flour 9 x 5 x 3 inch loaf pan.
Cream sugar and shortening. Add eggs and vanilla. Stir in flour,
baking powder, baking soda, and salt. Stir in apples and nuts. Spread
in pan. Mix 1 tablespoon sugar and 1/4 teaspoon cinnamon. Sprinkle
sugar/cinnamon mixture over batter. Bake at 350° F. for 50 to 60
minutes or until wooden pick inserted in center comes out clean.
Remove from pan immediately. Cool completely before slicing. Makes
1 loaf.

Sarah Brown
The Apple Works
Trafalgar, Indiana

Buckingham Orchards
Sunbury, Ohio

What started out to be a hobby with 20 apple trees planted in 1950 has turned into a major business for Dorothy and William Buckingham. After they were forced to relocate because of the construction of a federal dam, they decided to increase the size of their orchard. Many new and old-fashioned varieties were added.

Now there are about 125 varieties grown at the Buckingham Orchards. One of their best sellers is *Mutsu*, which they have been selling since 1967. They also provide school tours, cider making demonstrations, wagon rides, and pick-your-own in the fall.

APPLE-NUT LOAF

1/2 cup sugar
1/4 cup oil
2 eggs or 1/2 cup egg substitute
3 tablespoons sour milk
1 cup finely chopped unpared apple
1 teaspoon vanilla
2 cups flour
1 teaspoon baking powder
1/2 teaspoon baking soda
1/2 teaspoon salt
1/2 teaspoon cinnamon
1/4-1/2 cup chopped nuts

Mix together thoroughly sugar, oil, and eggs or egg substitute. Stir in sour milk, apple, and vanilla. Sift together dry ingredients. Stir into apple mixture. Blend in chopped nuts. Grease or spray a 9 x 5 loaf pan with nonstick cooking spray. Pour batter into prepared pan and let set for 20 minutes. Bake at 350° F. for 50 to 60 minutes or until loaf tests done.

"This slices more easily if it is wrapped after cooling and stored in the refrigerator about 24 hours, but it is delicious, although crumbly, warm from the oven."

Dorothy Buckingham
Buckingham Orchards
Sunbury, Ohio

Ski-Hi Fruit Farm

Baraboo, Wisconsin

Ski-Hi Fruit Farm has a long history of raising superior quality apples and fruit. The orchard's name was registered in 1915, however, the farm had been purchased much earlier, in 1907, by A.K. Bassett. It continues to remain in the Bassett family, producing many old and new apple varieties.

In addition to apples, the fall season finds many different produce gracing their sales area. This includes ornamental corn, gourds, grapes, pumpkins, squash, mum plants, and many others. It may be hard to decide what to buy with so many products from which to choose.

APPLE BOSTON BREAD

1/4 cup butter
1/3 cup honey
1/3 cup molasses
1 cup whole wheat flour
1 cup rye flour
1 cup cornmeal
2 teaspoons baking soda
1 teaspoon salt
2 cups buttermilk
2 cups coarsely chopped apples

Cream butter, honey, and molasses. Combine flours, cornmeal, baking soda, and salt; add to creamed mixture alternately with buttermilk. Fold in the apples. Spoon into two greased loaf pans. Bake at 325° F. for 1 hour. Cool for ten minutes before removing from the pans.

Olga Marie Bassett
Ski-Hi Fruit Farm
Baraboo, Wisconsin

Ski-Hi Fruit Farm

"IN THE HEART OF THE HILLS"

Masonic Homes Orchard
Elizabethtown, Pennsylvania

Masonic Homes Orchard was started in the early 1900's to supply the residents of the Masonic Homes retirement facility with fresh fruits and vegetables. Over the years, production has exceeded the needs of the Homes' residents. In the 1960's they expanded their operation into retail sales, providing quality products at competitive prices.

Today, many types of fruits and vegetables are grown, including over thirty varieties of apples. Their famous apple cider and fruit butters are available all year. White grape juice is used to sweeten their "no sugar added" apple butters. Mail order products include holiday gift boxes of fruit butters, citrus, and fruit.

APPLE KUCHEN

Kuchen
2 to 3 cups flour
1/3 cup sugar
1/2 teaspoon salt
1 package dry yeast
1/2 cup milk
1/4 cup butter
2 eggs
4 cups peeled and sliced apples

Topping
3/4 cup sugar
3 tablespoons flour
1/2 teaspoon cinnamon
2 tablespoons butter, softened

In large bowl, combine 1 cup flour, 1/3 cup sugar, salt, and yeast; blend well. In small saucepan, heat milk and 1/4 cup butter until very warm (120° F. To 130° F.). Add warm liquid and eggs to flour mixture. Blend at low speed with mixer until moistened. Beat 3 minutes at medium speed. By hand, stir in remainder 1 to 2 cups flour until dough pulls away, cleanly, from bowl. Generously grease 9 x 13 inch pan. On floured surface, knead dough lightly, until no longer sticky; press in greased pan. Arrange apple slices in rows on top of dough.

In small bowl, combine all topping ingredients; blend well. Sprinkle topping evenly over apples. Cover loosely with plastic wrap and cloth towel. Let rise in warm place (80° F. To 85° F.) until light, about 45 to 60 minutes. Heat oven to 375° F. Uncover dough. Bake 30 to 40 minutes, or until golden brown and apples are tender. Serve warm.

Tad E. Kuntz
Masonic Homes Orchard
Elizabethtown, Pennsylvania

Shultz Farm Foods
Athens, Tennessee

Wade and Cecileia Shultz and sons began to diversify their farming operation in the mid 1980's to include apples and vegetables. Their family started to make apple butter and jams in a kitchen constructed at the apple house. Later they added apple cider, apple brandy, dried apples, and other relish products made from their produce.

In the fall the Shultz's entertain with hayrides for schools and other special guests. *Arkansas Black* apples are one of their orchard's specialties.

APPLE BREAD

3 eggs
2 cups sugar
1 cup vegetable oil
2 cups grated apples
3 teaspoons vanilla
3 cups flour
1 teaspoon baking soda
1/4 teaspoon baking powder
1 teaspoon salt
3 teaspoons ground cinnamon

Beat eggs until light and foamy. Add sugar, oil, apples, and vanilla. Mix lightly, but well. Combine the flour, salt, soda, baking powder, and cinnamon. Add to the egg-apple mixture. Blend. Pour into two greased loaf pans, 9 x 5 x 3 inch. Bake in preheated oven for 1 hour at 350° F. Cool on rack.

"We sell this bread baked in small loaf pans at our roadside farm market.

Cecileia Shultz
Shultz Farm Foods
Athens, Tennessee

SALADS

Hollabaugh Bros., Inc.
Fruit Farms and Market
Biglerville, Pennsylvania

Hollabaugh Bros., Inc. is a family-owned and operated fruit farm and market with the third generation now taking an active role. They have a seasonal fruit market that caters to customers seeking a high-quality product. As a wholesale/retail outlet, they also offer gift packs/shipping and provide school tours. Each season they sponsor two festivals — a peach festival and an apple festival.

Specialty items at the Fruit Farm and Market include their own canned peaches available after August, and in the fall, their *Nittany* apple is getting very popular. This is an apple developed by Pennsylvania State University and named after the famous Nittany Lions.

APPLE COMPOTE

1 can (20 oz.) pineapple chunks
1/2 cup sugar
2 tablespoons cornstarch
1/3 cup orange juice
1 can (11 oz.) mandarin oranges, drained
4 apples, unpeeled, chopped
2 - 3 bananas
1 tablespoon lemon juice

Drain pineapple, reserving 3/4 cup juice. In a saucepan, combine sugar and cornstarch. Add pineapple juice, orange juice, and lemon juice. Cook and stir over medium heat until thickened and bubbly. Cook and stir one minute longer. Remove from the heat and set aside. In a bowl, combine pineapple chunks, oranges, apples, and bananas. Pour warm sauce over the fruit and stir gently to coat. Cover and refrigerate. Makes about 12 servings.

Kay E. Hollabaugh
Hollabaugh Bros., Inc.
Fruit Farms and Market
Biglerville, Pennsylvania

Schweizer Orchard

Amazonia, Missouri

Located along the bluffs of the Missouri River, Schweizer's Orchard location is favorable to growing many varieties of apples. Among the notables are their *Jonathan* apples, with the best flavor of any available. They also grow *Red* and *Golden Delicious, Grimes Golden, Rome, Winesap, Gala,* and *Jona Gold.*

The Schweizer Orchard has two retail locations, one is near St. Joseph and the other is in Amazonia. Both locations also sell honey, jellies, jams, sorghum, and cider.

QUICK APPLESAUCE SALAD

3 oz. package raspberry gelatin
1 1/2 cup boiling water
1 cup applesauce

Dissolve gelatin in water. Cool. Add applesauce and chill.

Recipe is reproduced with permission from Schweizer Orchards' information flyers given out at their retail locations.

Becky Schweizer
Schweizer Orchard
Amazonia, Missouri

The Ridge Orchards
Bourbon, Missouri

Some of the varieties in production at The Ridge include *Yellow Transparent, Lodi, Early Blaze, July Red, McIntosh, Macoun, Yellow Delicious, Rome, Jonathan, Cox Orange, Mutsu, Northern Spy, Sutton, Schwaar, York Imperial, Pumpkin Sweet, Somerset of Maine, Wolf River, Snow, Tompkins King, Pink Pearl, Lady, Red Delicious, Calville Blanc, Blue Pearmain,* and others. The Heitschs have noted that many apples develop full flavor after 3 to 4 years of bearing. They admonish others not to assume that the first apple crop is a true test of the variety.

A.B.C. SALAD
(Apple - Banana - Cabbage)

3 cups chopped apples
3 cups shredded cabbage
1 cup walnuts
1 banana, mashed
1 cup pineapple yogurt

Combine apples, cabbage and walnuts. Blend banana into yogurt. Lightly toss together.

Leona Heitsch
The Ridge Orchards
Bourbon, Missouri

45

Sanford's Sunset Orchards
Ellijay, Georgia

Sanford's Sunset Orchards were first started by the Howard Hyatt family in the 1950's. It was later purchased by the Caudell family in the 1970's and the Sanford family bought the orchard in 1985.

Several different kinds of apples are grown, such as *Red Delicious, Golden Delicious, Rome Beauty, Stayman, Winesap, Granny Smith, Gala, Yates, Arkansas Black, Mutsu,* and *Empire.* Sanfords make their own cider and apple butter. They generally have local farm products to sell along with their apples.

FRUIT AND RICE SALAD

2 cups cooked rice
1 (20 oz.) can crushed pineapple, drained
2 cups miniature marshmallows
1/2 cup sugar
3 medium apples, cubed
(*Red* or *Golden Delicious*)
1/2 cup diced maraschino cherries
1 cup heavy cream, whipped

Combine cooked rice, pineapples, marshmallows, and sugar in large bowl. Toss gently to mix. Cover and refrigerate at least 3 hours. Fold in apples and cherries. Fold in whipped cream. Chill for 1 hour or more before serving.

Eulene Sanford
Sanford's Sunset Orchards
Ellijay, Georgia

Irons' Fruit Farm
Lebanon, Ohio

Irons' Fruit Farm is located midway between Cincinnati and Dayton, Ohio and is 15 minutes north of **Paramount's Kings Island** amusement park. Lebanon is known for having Ohio's oldest inn, **The Golden Lamb Inn.** This restaurant uses apples and cider from Irons' Fruit Farm. The last Saturday of September is Lebanon's "Applefest."

The orchard was started in the early 1940's, however, the farm has been in the family for over 100 years. It is now in the 4th generation, being managed by Ron and Gayle Irons and son, Bill. They grow 30 acres of apples, including *Lodi, Paulared, Gala, Rambo, Idared, Red* and *Gold Delicious, McIntosh, Jonathan, Melrose, Stayman,* and *Winesap.*

DOUBLE APPLE SALAD

1 cup boiling water
3 oz. package orange gelatin
1 cup apple cider
1 cup chopped apple
1/4 cup diced celery
1/4 cup chopped walnuts
Dash of salt (to 1/2 teaspoon)

Pour boiling water over orange gelatin and salt; stir to dissolve. Add cider; chill until partially set. Stir in chopped apple, celery, and walnuts. Spoon into 3-cup ring mold. Chill until set.

"This salad has been served a lot at Thanksgiving dinners on our farm and also at Ohio's oldest Inn here in Lebanon, Ohio, **The Golden Lamb.** *"*

Gayle Irons
Irons' Fruit Farm
Lebanon, Ohio

Mincer Orchard

Hamburg, Iowa

The loess hills upon which the Mincers have planted fruit trees get their name from the German word for "wind blown soil." Only in these parts of North America can the unusual and picturesque hills be seen.

Mincer Orchard was planted over 100 years ago by Charles Taylor, great-grandfather of the present owners, Mr. and Mrs. Ed Mincer. The elder Taylor came to the Hamburg area by covered wagon from Thorntown, Indiana. Under his management, fruit trees flourished on the rich, virgin, Iowa soil. Ribbons and trophies were awarded to the excellent fruit, which was shown at fairs held throughout the midwest. At the turn of the century, boxcars loaded with barrels of apples were shipped to Chicago markets.

Four main apples indigenous to this region are grown — *Red* and *Golden Delicious*, *Jonathan*, and *Winesap*. The Mincers also grow many old and new varieties for their customers to taste and enjoy.

Mincer Orchard has always been and continues to be a family operation. Mr. and Mrs. Mincer are proud to start the second one hundred years with the pledge to continue growing the finest fruits and fruit products for customer satisfaction.

APPLE SALAD

3-oz. package lemon gelatin
1 cup boiling water
1 cup pineapple juice
4 cups grated raw apples
1/2 cup grated cheese
8 oz. can crushed pineapple, drained
1 cup small marshmallows
1 package whipped topping, prepared

Dissolve gelatin in boiling water. Add pineapple juice. Chill until thick and syrupy. Add apples, cheese, pineapple, marshmallows, and whipped topping. Pour into 9 x 13 inch pan. Chill 2 to 3 hours. Serves 12.

Ed Mincer
Mincer Orchard
Hamburg, Iowa

Schreiman Orchard
Waverly, Missouri

The 20 mile river bluff region between Lexington and Waverly, where the Schreiman Orchards are located, grows nearly half of the apples in Missouri. The fertile loess soil, almost 100 feet deep, gives these apples a flavor all their own, different from any other apples grown in the country. Large areas of loess soil are found mostly along the Rhine River in Germany, the Yang-tse-Kiang River in China, and along parts of the Missouri River.

Judy Schreiman Marshall's pioneer uncles cleared the virgin land in the 1920's before planting the original apple orchard. Jim and Judy Marshall, the present owners, still have the original maps and journals of the everyday work done in the orchard at that time, which is much like that of the present day. Mrs. Marshall's parents began growing peaches, in addition to apples, in the 50's, 60's, and 70's. Since then, the orchard has been replanted several times.

APPLE PICKERS' FAVORITE APPLE SALAD

1 3-oz. package red gelatin
1 cup hot water
1 16-oz. can whole cranberries
1 20-oz. can crushed pineapple, drained
2 oranges, diced
2 apples, diced
1 cup chopped pecans

Dissolve gelatin in hot water. Add cranberries. Let cool slightly, then mix in fruit and nuts.

"My sister-in-law's family in St. Louis has this at Thanksgiving. It's great!"

Judy Schreiman Marshall
Schreiman Orchards
Waverly, Missouri

Vaughn Orchard and Country Store

Weston, Missouri

Located near historic Weston, Missouri, where apples and tobacco reign supreme, Vaughn Orchard and Country Store offer a wide array of apple products. Owned by Walter and L. R. Vaughn, the orchard began retailing apples in a tobacco barn in 1970. Now there are 54 acres of apples, which were planted in 1960.

Many new services have been added the last few years. These include making cider, apple butter, and cider jelly on the premises. On weekends in the fall a big smoker for barbecues is going. A haunted barn greets visitors in October. Wagon rides are available for trips through the orchards. The Country Store features a wide assortment of apple-related, as well as other unique gifts and food items.

WALDORF SALAD

3-oz. package gelatin
(red, apple, or lemon flavor)
2 cups Vaughn apple cider
1 cup chopped apple
1 cup chopped celery
1/2 cup chopped walnuts
8 oz. cream cheese
2 tablespoons mayonnaise

Follow gelatin directions, using cider instead of water. Thicken slightly. Fold in apple, celery, and nuts. Chill until firm in 9 inch square pan. Mix softened cream cheese with mayonnaise until spreadable. Spread on top of gelatin.

Vaughn Orchard and Country Store
Weston, Missouri

Ochs Orchard
Warwick, New York

Ochs Orchard is a three generation family farm. In the late 1930's it was owned and managed through the partnership of Ochs & Scheuermann. Peter Ochs and Chris Scheuermann ran a wholesale apple and peach fruit farm until 1969. Peter Ochs bought out his partner and in 1971, Leslie (his son) began to operate the orchard.

In 1973, Leslie and his wife, Susan, bought the farm from Peter and began promoting the retail trade by opening a farmstand. They also began growing vegetables to have more variety of produce for sale. Pick-Your-Own-Apples was started and became very successful. Eventually, a cider press was installed and fresh cider was made every week.

OCHS' WALDORF SALAD

1 *Red Delicious* apple
1 stalk celery
1/4 cup walnut pieces
1/4 cup cheddar cheese
3 tablespoons mayonnaise

Optional additions:
1/4 cup chicken or
1/4 cup raisins or
1/4 cup flaked tuna or
1/4 cup hard-cooked eggs

Quarter apple but do not peel. Cut out core and cube. Cut celery into small pieces. Cube cheese. Mix all ingredients together, adding more mayonnaise, if desired. Makes 2 servings.

Susan Ochs
Ochs Orchard
Warwick, New York

Buckingham Orchards

Sunbury, Ohio

Trends change for apple growers, just as changes occur in other businesses. This is evident in the operation of Buckingham Orchards, as they currently tend to be focusing on combining farming with entertainment. Their fastest growing business segment is "pick-your-own", when people come from far and near for an adventure in the great outdoors. The Apple Blossom festival in May and the fall cider making demonstrations also bring folks in for traditional events that help to celebrate the goodness of the fruit.

BUCKINGHAM'S WALDORF SLAW

Cabbage
Red-skinned apples
Celery
1/3 cup raisins
Marzetti's Slaw Dressing™ or
Miracle Whip™

Shred cabbage finely to make 2 cups. Dice or chop red-skinned apples to make 1 cup (do not peel apples). Thinly slice celery to make 1/3 cup. Blend ingredients together and add raisins. Add salad dressing to taste.

"To cut calories, thin the dressing with equal parts orange juice and milk. Add about 2 tablespoons sugar and ½ to 1 teaspoon salt. This is a delicious variation of cole slaw and is especially good with pork or sausage meals."

Dorothy Buckingham
Buckingham Orchards
Sunbury, Ohio

The following is excerpted from **RECIPES FROM FAMILY, FRIENDS, AND NEIGHBORS OF SCHREIMAN ORCHARDS** *and published with permission from Schreiman Orchards, Waverly, Missouri.*

LIFE AT THE ORCHARD

It is not quite 6:00 a.m. Dawn is just breaking over the hills near the Missouri River so it isn't really hot yet, only about 90°. The air is heavy. A cool breeze would be welcome.

By 9:00 the heat can be suffocating for pickers, but the fruit just keeps getting juicier and sweeter. The ones way at the top in the hottest sun are the largest and reddest of all — worth a trip back up the ladder for one big one missed. As the pickers move slowly down the row, they watch for the row to grow shorter. Their trucks leave tracks through the dew damp grass and their shoes are soaked as if it had rained.

A couple of full pick-up loads will be enough to start selling so some of the pickers can head back to the roadside market. It sets in a section of the apple orchard first planted in the twenties. Facing north, the big, white barn-type market is like a breath of fresh air as neighbors and travelers begin calling and coming to check on the day's picking.

Some want a small basket of big fancy picturesque fruit to be eaten immediately. Others search among the rows of baskets to find the best bargain to make into pies, or to can for their cellar. Many bring recipes to share. Others have questions about how to preserve the fruit they buy. Yes, another day at the orchard has just begun.

MAIN DISHES

THANKSGIVING

by Leona Heitsch of The Ridge Orchards, Bourbon, Missouri from
Echos of the Ridge, centering on the history of northern Washington
County, Missouri

In those days of spring
when I was young
and moving fast
I sometimes took the time
to wonder why
a man just finished
with a day's orchard work
would return
after the evening meal
and walk among apple trees
until dusk.

Now,
at the end of November,
I walk through the twilight
in awe of the fullness
of next year's buds,
grateful for the life and strength
in the newly grafted wood
Dad chose with me
from a few old apple trees
left at the edges
of our orchard-gone
to suburb.

It is enough
to re-create
in this new place
the fruitful hills of home.

BREAKFAST APPLES

8 to 10 tree ripened apples, sliced (not peeled)
1 teaspoon cinnamon
1 cup water
1 to 2 cups oatmeal
Honey or maple syrup sweetener (not necessary as tree ripe fruit is really sweet)

Place apples in frying pan and add one cup water. Cook gently on stovetop until apples are tender. Add cinnamon. Place apples in four bowls and top with 1/4 to 1/2 cup of uncooked oatmeal, either quick or old fashioned, according to your taste. Makes 4 servings.

"This has surprised our guests with its simplicity and its tastiness and good old fashioned stick-to-your-ribs staying power. By shifting from conventional breakfasts to this, we have personally lost weight and kept it off, with no problems of hunger pangs and snacking between meals."

Leona and Charles Heitsch
The Ridge Orchards
Bourbon, Missouri

63

The Apple Barn at Hope Orchards

Hope, Maine

Each year, many visitors are drawn to this orchard, attracted by the closeness to the ocean and the tasty fruit grown by Karl and Linda Dreschsler. A retail store is open late August until Christmas.

CHICKEN CAPRICE

4 pieces of chicken
1 tablespoon oil
2 cups applesauce
(*McIntosh*, good choice)
1/2 cup apple juice or cider
2 tablespoons lemon juice
1/2 cup brown sugar
1 teaspoon mustard
1/2 cup slivered almonds (optional)

In electric skillet, brown chicken on both sides in oil. Combine all the other ingredients. Pour applesauce mixture over chicken. Cook about 45 minutes. Turn chicken; spoon sauce over chicken. Cook another 15 minutes, or until done.

Linda and Karl Drechsler
The Apple Barn at Hope Orchards
Hope, Maine

Anderson Farm Orchard
Zion, Illinois

Apples and fresh pressed cider are the featured products at Anderson Farm Orchard. Apple varieties include *McIntosh, Gala, Jonathan, Cortland, Jonalicious, Red* and *Golden Delicious, Rome Beauty, Earliblaze, Snowapple,* and *Winesap.*

Anderson Farm Orchard is owned by John Anderson, Bob Grulke, and Bob Fink. It is open for business from September to November, 7 days a week.

APPLESAUCE MEATLOAF

1 lb. ground beef
1 egg, beaten
2 tablespoons chopped onion
1 teaspoon salt
1/2 cup bread or cracker crumbs
1/2 cup applesauce
2 tablespoons catsup

Combine ingredients and mix well. Put in a greased loaf pan. Spread catsup on top of loaf. Bake at 350° F. for 1 hour or until done. Serve with additional applesauce.

Anderson Farm Orchard
Zion, Illinois

Stark Brothers Nurseries and Orchards Company
Louisiana, Missouri

The history of Stark Brothers Nurseries and Orchards Company spans almost 200 years of growing and continually testing fruits and production methods. It began in 1816, when James Hart Stark chose an area for his first home just west of the Mississippi, in the rolling fertile hills of Missouri, near the town of what is now called Louisiana. This site gave him a good view of the surrounding countryside, and it looked like a good place for an orchard, for he had brought with him apple scions from his father's farm in Bourbon County, Kentucky. He went to work building a cabin and clearing the land. Planting his orchard was second in importance only to a roof over his head for his wife and young son.

James Hart Stark learned the rare art of budding and grafting to get better fruit trees from his father, Captain James Stark in Kentucky. The apple scions he brought with him in his saddle bags were very important to him, but little did he dream of their enduring legacy. The scions, which, when grafted to wild crab apple trees, would grow some of the first cultivated fruit west of the Mississippi, and his fruit culture would spread eventually throughout the world.

The English had developed an apple known as the *Jeniton,* which was probably the first variety of apple planted by young Stark. Since the early settlers brought with them apples from England, the early types were probably ones propagated there. It was in England that selective breeding of apples first became a science.

Mr. Stark continued to plant orchards scientifically, carefully selecting, grafting, and keeping only the most superior fruit varieties. Soon his trees became recognized for their exceptional quality and people traveled great distances for grafted and budded trees.

APPLE SAUSAGE ROLL

1 pound sausage
2 cups diced apples
2 cups bread crumbs
1 small onion, diced

On waxed paper, roll out sausage into a rectangle 1/2 inch thick. Combine apples, bread crumbs, and onion; spread over meat. Roll as for jelly roll. Place in 9 x 13 inch baking dish. Bake at 350° F. for 45 minutes.

Rose Marie Buchholz
Louisiana, Missouri

CHILL REQUIRED
by Leona Heitsch

This ice on branch
...salubrious! It stirs
a crisp, essential
nudge to apple cells.

Deep in these buds
and deep in roots
it's working now.

Day by day,
by increments,
will grow the winter's
span of chill
required to fill
these frozen branches with
the bloom of spring
the growth of summer,
the green, the gold,
the crimson
fruitfulness of fall.

ACCOMPANIMENTS

Schweizer Orchard
Amazonia, Missouri

During the early 1900's, Missouri was the top apple producing state in the nation. It was during this time that the Schweizer Orchard was established by Conrad F. Schweizer in the rolling hills of Missouri near Amazonia. Originally, both fruit and berries were harvested and packed. Today, however, only fall varieties of apples are grown and packed. The orchard is now operated by the third generation of the same family.

MICROWAVE APPLESAUCE

8 medium cooking apples
1/2 cup water
1 cup sugar
Dash cinnamon, optional

Peel, core, and quarter apples. Place in 2 quart dish. Cover and microwave on High 10-12 minutes until apples are tender, stirring once. Stir in sugar. Let set 2-3 minutes to dissolve sugar. For a smoother applesauce, blend in blender.

Recipe is reprinted with permission from Schweizer Orchards' informational flyer given out at their retail locations.

Becky Schweizer
Schweizer Orchard
Amazonia, Missouri

Vaughn Orchard and Country Store

Weston, Missouri

Take a drive just off Interstate 29 to the historic town of Weston, Missouri and stop at the busy apple hub —Vaughn Orchard and Country Store. Smell the apple butter cooking and watch as it bubbles in their Crabapple Shanty. Join the Vaughns for a memorable apple choosing session and other shopping delights at their Country Store.

FRIED JONATHANS

6 peeled and cored *Jonathan* apples
Scant 1/2 cup sugar
1 teaspoon cinnamon
2 tablespoons cinnamon red hots
1/2 stick butter

Melt butter in heavy skillet. Sauté apples until transparent. Sprinkle sugar/cinnamon mixture, and red hots over apples. Stir until melted.

"Serve warm with vanilla ice cream as dessert—over waffles with sausage as a Sunday night supper—or as a condiment with pork chops."

Vaughn Orchard and Country Store
Weston, Missouri

The Apple Core Orchard
Durand, Michigan

The Apple Core Orchard is well known in the Durand, Michigan area for its excellent cider. Good cider is a product of proper blending of apple varieties, clean apples, and sanitary equipment.

Tours for 15 to 50 people are a specialty of the Apple Core Orchard. The tour includes a hay ride, nature walk, refreshments, and music. October is their Autumn Extravaganza Month, featuring a different event each weekend.

The original orchard was established in the 1940's by John and Ruth Drury. The establishment was a 40 acre tract of land located near Durand, Michigan — the railroad hub of Michigan. In the early 1970's, a store was built and named "Drury's Farm Market."

In 1979 the farm was purchased by Stan and Marilyn Turner, who were both teaching school at the time. The name of the business was changed to "The Apple Core Orchard." Since retirement, the Turners have directed all their energy and talents into making the orchard a fun and educational place for all to visit.

72

CANDIED APPLES
(Red Apples)

1 1/2 cups water
1 1/2 cups sugar
1/2 cup cinnamon red hot candy
3 or 4 drops red food coloring (optional)
4 large *Spy* apples, peeled, cored, and
    cut in half

Put water, sugar, cinnamon red hots and food coloring in large 4 quart pan. Stir while bringing to a boil. Continue stirring and boil about 10 minutes or until red hots melt. This should begin to form a light syrup.

Add apples and cook on medium heat with lid for 10 minutes. Carefully turn apples over and cook another 10 or 15 minutes, until apples are tender. Place in serving dish and pour remaining syrup over apples. You may drop miniature marshmallows on top while still hot. Cool. Refrigerate and serve cold.

"This recipe is written down for the first time. It was handed down to me by my mother by just watching her make it. It is a family tradition —always served on Thanksgiving and Christmas or special occasions. At our house it is known as 'Red Apples'."

Marilyn Turner
The Apple Core Orchard
Durand, Michigan

Buckingham Orchards

Sunbury, Ohio

The farm market at Buckingham Orchards is housed in a rehabilitated barn dating from about 1830. The building was literally turned inside-out, as they used the exterior siding on the inside walls. The old weathered boards have given the interior a unique character. All of the original beams and structural members were retained just as the original owner left them. The exterior of the market shows the original lines of the barn. The reconstructed barn serves as an ideal backdrop for their country products.

STUFFED CRYSTALLIZED APPLES

3 1/2 cups water
3 1/2 cups sugar
2 teaspoons lemon juice
8 small *Red Delicious* apples
1/2 teaspoon red food coloring
3 oz. cream cheese
1/4 cup chopped nuts

Two days before using: boil water, sugar, and lemon juice in a heavy pan or Dutch oven for 30 minutes. Peel and core the apples. Lower them into syrup, after adding the red color. Boil apples uncovered moderately fast so the syrup bubbles up around them —about 15 minutes. Turn apples and cook until transparent — may take about 35 minutes. Remove from heat; cover; let stand 30 minutes. Transfer apples to plate; spoon syrup over and refrigerate, uncovered until time to serve. At serving time, soften cream cheese, mix in nuts, and stuff centers of apples. Garnish with parsley, watercress, or celery curls. Makes 8 very elegant garnishes.

"This recipe is a bit troublesome and time-consuming, but the results are worth it!"

Dorothy Buckingham
Buckingham Orchards
Sunbury, Ohio

Herndon Orchard

Marionville, Missouri

Bob and Sara Herndon of Herndon Orchard near Marionville,
Missouri raise many varieties of apples and make a great tasting apple
cider. In fact, they attained the honor of being No. 1 in cider making
at the Missouri State Horticulture show and were 1st runner up in the
9-Midwest States, held at the Illinois Horticulture show in 1995.

The Marionville area has five small orchards now, but in the
1940's, it was the apple capital of Missouri. Sara Herndon's father
purchased the existing property in 1946. Later, in 1954, a retail
market was built and opened on a new highway. Sara and Bob learned
the trade as apprentices, beginning in 1958. In conjunction with their
apple business, each year they give free tours to 450 local school
children.

CHEESE AND APPLES

8 - 10 medium cooking apples
1 cup flour
1 cup sugar
1/2 cup butter or margarine
12 oz. grated cheddar cheese

Peel and slice apples. Cook gently in small amount of water until tender. Spray 9 x 12 inch pan with nonstick cooking spray. Stir together flour and sugar. Cut in butter or margarine to make a crumbly mixture. Add cheese. Place half of the apples in baking pan. Cover with 1/2 of the dry ingredients. Repeat. Bake at 350° F. for 30 to 40 minutes or until golden brown. Serve warm or cold. Yield: 16-20 servings.

Sara Herndon
Herndon Orchard
Marionville, Missouri

Louisburg Cider Mill
Louisburg, Kansas

Louisburg Cider Mill opened its doors on September 2, 1977. Previously, standing on that site, was one weary, abandoned hay barn, alone in a Kansas field. Now renovated, the 120-year-old classic is the hallmark of their business.

Throughout the years, Tom and Shelly Schierman have enhanced their basic structure and have concentrated on making apple cider the old fashioned way — with a rack and fruit cloth press. Even though their cider making method dates back 2000 years, it still produces the best quality juice. Their press was built in Connecticut in the early 1900's. They use a special blend of *Jonathan, Red* and *Golden Delicious, Winesap*, and *Rome Beauty* apples. Apples are bought from commercial growers, mostly north of them along the Missouri River from about St. Joseph to Waverly.

APPLE AND CHEESE STRUDEL

1 pound apples, peeled, cored, diced
(*Jonathan*, good choice)
2 tablespoons lemon juice
1 teaspoon dried thyme
1/2 teaspoon ground nutmeg
8 ounces Roquefort cheese, crumbled
3/4 cup roasted walnuts, chopped
1/2 teaspoon ground black pepper
1/2 cup melted butter
3/4 cup dried bread crumbs
4 large sheets filo pastry

Preheat oven to 190° F. Toss diced apples in a bowl with next six ingredients. Grease a 12 inch square baking sheet. Place one sheet of filo pastry on baking sheet, brush with melted butter, sprinkle with 1/3 of bread crumbs. Work quickly and keep unused pastry covered with a damp cloth. Layer the filo sheets, brush each with melted butter, sprinkle with bread crumbs. Do not sprinkle crumbs on top layer.

Drain the juices from apple/cheese filling. Spoon the filling along one side of the filo to within 2 inches of the long edges. Fold the long edges over the filling, then fold the end flap over to enclose the filling. Gently roll up the strudel so the seam side is underneath. Brush with melted butter. Bake for 30 minutes in 190° F. oven until pastry is golden and apples are tender.

Shelly Schierman
Louisburg Cider Mill, Inc.
Louisburg, Kansas

CIDER BASTING FOR TURKEY

1/2 cup butter, melted
1 cup hard cider
1 cup orange juice
1/2 cup lemon juice
1/2 teaspoon crushed basil

Melt butter in a pan. Add 1 cup hard cider (fresh cider will turn hard if left unrefrigerated for 2 to 3 days), juices, and basil. Cook over low heat until well dissolved.

"This can be used to baste a whole turkey or a turkey breast when baking —also good for moistening turkey stuffing. Adds a wonderful flavor to gravy as well!"

Shelly Schierman
Louisburg Cider Mill, Inc.
Louisburg, Kansas

The Homestead Orchard
Salem, Ohio

Working in harmony with their surroundings, James and Mary Kirk raise certified organic fruit and hay. They grow about 12 different varieties of tree fruits, including apples, peaches, pears, plums, and nectarines, all without the use of chemical insecticides. They believe in being "friends to the land."

In commenting about their work, the Kirks exclaimed: "We are rewarded every day and excited about the future!"

APPLE STUFFING

4 tablespoons bacon fat
2 cups tart apples, diced and unpeeled
2 teaspoons sugar or honey
1/2 cup dry bread crumbs
1/4 teaspoon nutmeg
1/4 teaspoon cinnamon
1/4 cup chopped walnuts, optional

Melt bacon fat in a large skillet. Add apples and sugar and cook over medium heat for 5 minutes, stirring constantly. Remove from heat and toss in the crumbs and spices. Add nuts, if desired. Yield: 2 1/2 cups.

"A fine Christmas stuffing, excellent for all poultry as well as veal and pork."

James and Mary Kirk
The Homestead Orchard
Salem, Ohio

Sanford's Sunset Orchards
Ellijay, Georgia

People from several states stop at Sanford's Sunset Orchards each fall during September and October when they are open. Local farm products are generally sold along with their apples.

The Jimmy Sanford family gives orchard tours for the schools attended by their grandsons. They enjoy meeting and talking with their customers and, as Mrs. Sanford says, "We have made many new friends this way."

APPLES AND SWEET POTATO BAKE

2 cups apples, peeled and sliced
(*Golden Delicious* or *Rome Beauty)*
2 cups cooked and sliced sweet potatoes
1/2 cup brown sugar
1/2 cup raisins
1/2 cup butter or margarine
Dash of nutmeg and cinnamon

Layer half the apples, sweet potatoes, brown sugar, and raisins in 1 1/2 quart casserole dish. Sprinkle with spices. Repeat with remaining half. Dot with butter or margarine. Cover and bake at 350° F. for 30 minutes. Uncover and bake until apples are soft and top is brown.

Eulene Sanford
Sanford's Sunset Orchards
Ellijay, Georgia

APPLE CHEESE CASSEROLE

1/2 cup flour
1/2 cup sugar
1/4 teaspoon salt
1/4 cup butter or margarine
7 apples, peeled, cored and sliced
(*Golden Delicious*, good choice)
1/3 cup water
1 tablespoon lemon juice
1 cup shredded cheddar cheese

Combine flour, sugar, and salt. Mix well. Cut in butter or margarine until mixture resembles coarse meal. Toss apples with water and lemon juice. Spoon into greased 8-inch casserole dish and sprinkle with flour mixture. Bake uncovered at 350° F. for 30 minutes. Top with cheese and bake for 5 minutes.

Eulene Sanford
Sanford's Sunset Orchards
Ellijay, Georgia

Irons' Fruit Farm
Lebanon, Ohio

   With the harvest at its fullest and the shelves brimming with good food, this is indeed the best time of the year at Irons' Fruit Farm. The farm bakery operates June through December. Cider donuts, apple pies, fritters, dumplings, and turnovers are featured in September and October. About 30 to 35 people help through mid-September to late October in a variety of jobs. Apple cider, as well as apple butter, jams, and jellies are made in the fall through February. The holiday season finds everyone busy making fruit/gift baskets and boxes.

APPLE CIDER SAUCE

2 cups cider
1 cup sugar
1 tablespoon cornstarch
2 tablespoons lemon juice
1 teaspoon pumpkin pie spice

Cook and stir until thick. Add 1 tablespoon butter and stir until melted.

"Great on pancakes!"

Gayle Irons
Irons' Fruit Farm
Lebanon, Ohio

BARBECUE SAUCE

Blend:
1 cup Catalina dressing
1 cup ketchup
1 cup apple butter

Gayle Irons
Irons' Fruit Farm
Lebanon, Ohio

ORION IN THE OZARKS

by Leona Heitsch of The Ridge Orchards, Bourbon,
Missouri
from **Echos of the Ridge**

Whoever named
our belted midnight guide
and conjured up a dog
to go beside
is lost somewhere in time
where no man now
can catch his zeal
for creaturing a screen
so curved and wide
that he could cause it to reveal
the mind of man
and all the imagery inside.

Unless,
some autumn night
a hunter of today
should slow his pace
and wait on a persimmon ridge
to hear Orion's missiles
dropping out of space.

COOKIES

The Apple Works
Trafalgar, Indiana

About 65 varieties of apples are grown at The Apple Works. These include such antiques as *Newtown Pippin, Esopus Spitzenberg* (Thomas Jefferson's favorite apple) and *Golden Russet. Newtown Pippin* is the oldest commercially grown apple native to the United States, and said to have been favored by George Washington. *Golden Russet* was marketed commercially in the early 1800s.

Many newer varieties are also grown, such as *Gala, Fuji, Jonagold, and. Jonamac. Gala,* developed in New Zealand and introduced in the 1960s, is a cross between *Golden Delicious* and J.H. Kidd's *Orange Red. Fuji* is a good keeping apple, retaining its firmness for up to a year if refrigerated. *Jonagold* is, as one might imagine, a cross between *Jonathan* and *Golden Delicious*, whereas *Jonamac* is a cross between *Jonathan* and *McIntosh*.

GLAZED APPLE COOKIES

1 1/3 cups brown sugar, packed
1/2 cup butter or margarine
1 egg
2 cups flour
1 teaspoon baking soda
1/2 teaspoon salt
1 teaspoon ground cinnamon
1/4 teaspoon ground cloves
1/4 teaspoon gound nutmeg
1 cup chopped nuts
1 cup raisins
1 1/2 cups grated apples, peeling is optional

Glaze
1 1/2 cups confectioners' sugar
2 tablespoons milk
1 tablespoon softened butter or margarine
1/2 teaspoon vanilla

Pre-heat oven to 400° F. Beat brown sugar with butter or margarine until creamed. Add egg and beat until fluffy. Combine dry ingredients and add gradually to creamed mixture. Add apples, nuts, and raisins. Drop by rounded tablespoons unto a greased cookie sheet. Bake at 400° F. for about 10 minutes.

Prepare glaze and mix until smooth. Spread on cookies while still warm. Makes 3 dozen cookies.

Sarah Brown
The Apple Works
Trafalgar, Indiana

Alasa Farms
Alton, New York

Alasa Farms is the site of a former Shaker settlement. During the summer a Shaker festival is held in the area as well as many antique shows.

Purchased in 1924, Alasa Farms now grow 50 acres of apples, along with 20 acres of hay. They offer pick-your-own fruit in October. Tours are given year around for bus and school groups.

AMY QUACKENBUSH'S GLAZED FRESH APPLE COOKIES

2 cups flour
1/2 teaspoon salt
1 teaspoon baking soda
1/2 cup soft shortening
1 1/3 cups brown sugar
1 teaspoon cinnamon
1 teaspoon ground cloves
1/2 teaspoon nutmeg
1 egg
1 cup chopped nuts
1 cup raisins, optional
1/4 cup milk or apple juice
1 cup chopped apples (any variety)

Heat oven to 400° F. Combine flour, baking soda, and salt. Set aside. Mix shortening, brown sugar, cinnamon, cloves, nutmeg, and egg until blended. Stir in half of flour mixture, then nuts, apples, and raisins. Blend in milk (or apple juice), then remaining flour mixture. Drop rounded teaspoons of dough on greased cookie sheet. Bake at 400° F. for 11-14 minutes or until done. While cookies are warm, spread with *Vanilla Glaze*.

Vanilla Glaze
Blend 1 1/2 cups confectioners' sugar with 1 tablespoon soft butter or margarine, 1/4 teaspoon vanilla, 1/8 teaspoon salt, and 2 1/2 tablespoons milk.

Makes 3-4 dozen cookies.

Alasa Farms
Alton, New York

Cold Hollow Cider Mill

Waterbury Center, Vermont

   In 1974, in the hamlet of Bakersfield, Vermont, Eric and Francine Chittenden pressed their first batch of cider. Entering the cider business was an attempt to make their farm produce a living.

   Being in the foothills of the Cold Hollow mountains, they chose that name for their new venture. Developing the mill in those early years and establishing the mill's presence in Northern Vermont was an exciting time. By the end of the second season they were servicing scores of stores, restaurants, and schools with fresh cider. Wanting to expand their business, the Chittendens moved to Waterbury Center in the summer of 1976. Since then, they have added a bakery, a mail order business, and a gift shop that highlights Vermont products.

APPLE CHEDDAR SCONES

4 cups whole wheat pastry flour
2/3 cup maple sugar granules
2 tablespoons baking powder
1 teaspoon salt
4 eggs
1 cup yogurt
1 cup butter
1 diced apple
2 ounces grated cheddar cheese

Combine flour, maple sugar granules, baking powder, and salt.
Add remaining ingredients and mix. Form into 12 rounds and place on
greased cookie sheet. Flatten and brush on egg wash (1 egg beaten
with 2 teaspoons water). Bake in preheated oven at 350° F. for 20
minutes or until brown.

Gail McCain
Cold Hollow Cider Mill
Waterbury Center, Vermont

Honey Hill Orchard
Waterman, Illinois

Kathy Bock's parents, Harold and Edna Askelson, planted their first apple trees in 1965 as a hobby. In 1977, they turned it into a business and Kathy and her husband, Steve, joined them.

The old farm barn at the Orchard was converted into the Apple Sales Barn, complete with a "Feeding Trough", where they serve homemade cider donuts, apple pie, and caramel apples. A farm petting zoo and wagon rides are available on weekends during apple season.

CARAMEL APPLE BARS

1/2 cup softened butter or margarine
1/4 cup shortening
1 cup brown sugar
1 3/4 cups flour
1 cup rolled oats
1/2 teaspoon baking soda
1 teaspoon salt
1/2 cup chopped pecans
4 1/2 cups peeled, chopped apples
3 tablespoons flour
14 ounce package caramels
3 tablespoons butter or margarine

Cream butter or margarine, shortening, and brown sugar until fluffy. Add flour, oats, baking soda, and salt. Mix well. Stir in pecans. Reserve 2 cups. Press remaining oat mixture into the bottom of a 9 x 13 inch baking pan. Toss apples with 3 tablespoons flour. Spoon over oat mixture in pan. Melt caramels and 3 tablespoons butter or margarine over low heat. Drizzle over apples. Top with reserved oat mixture. Bake at 400° F. for 25 to 30 minutes. Cool before serving.

"We like to warm individual servings of these bars in the microwave and then top with ice cream."

Steve and Kathy Bock
Honey Hill Orchard
Waterman, Illinois

Shatzer Fruit Market and Orchards

Chambersburg, Pennsylvania

Shatzer Orchards are located in historic Franklin County in the heart of the Cumberland Valley, 25 miles from Gettysburg Battlefield. Ninety acres of fruit orchards are grown, containing sweet cherries, peaches, plums, pears, apples, sweet corn, pumpkins, gourds, and Indian corn. All fruits are hand picked and hand sorted and graded before being sold in their market.

Pride in growing and displaying quality fruit is evident. Shatzer Fruit Market received the No. 1 Award at the Pennsylvania State Farm Show in January 1995 for having the best fruit market display in the show.

The orchards are now owned by Jack and Wilma Mickey and their son, Dwight. They were owned by Wilma's great uncle, W. O. Bingham, from 1934 until 1945, however, parts of the orchard were established much earlier. Wilma's parents, Edison and Martha Shatzer, were the owners until 1971 at which time Wilma and Jack took over the business.

Shatzer's farm has a weather station serving Pennsylvania State University that records weather conditions for spraying and other information helpful for the orchard industry. They were one of the first in their county to use insect traps commercially for insect count to cut down on the use of chemicals.

This is a family business that takes pride in caring for the land — always realizing the importance family farms have on the future well-being of the country. Their interest is in keeping the land sustainable so as to continue producing America's bounty and nourishing its people.

APPLE BROWNIES

1/2 cup shortening
1 cup sugar
1/2 teaspoon vanilla
2 eggs, beaten
1 cup flour, sifted
1 teaspoon baking powder
1/2 teaspoon salt
1 teaspoon cinnamon
1 1/2 cups finely grated apple
1/2 cup chopped nuts, optional

Melt shortening and beat in sugar and vanilla. Stir in eggs; sift dry
ingredients and mix in. Stir in apples and nuts. Spread in greased 9
inch square pan. Bake at 350° F. for 30-35 minutes. Cut while warm
into 2 inch squares. Makes about 16 brownies.

Wilma Shatzer Mickey
Shatzer Fruit Market & Orchards
Chambersburg, Pennsylvania

Diehl's Orchard and Cider Mill
Holly, Michigan

The Diehl family has owned and operated an orchard and farm market since 1954. Started by Paul and Isabelle Diehl, it is now run by their children and grandchildren. Current managers are Sally and Jack Diehl, their son, Mike Diehl, and niece Sue Diehl Burton.

There are now 75 acres of apples and plums on the farm. A cider mill was added to the business in 1957 and upgraded in 1968.

Cider will keep for an extended period of time if kept just over 32 degrees Fahrenheit. If frozen in plastic jugs, it will keep for a year or more, just remember to take out a cup of cider to allow for expansion while freezing.

APPLE BUTTER BARS

1 1/2 cups flour
1 teaspoon baking soda
1 teaspoon salt
2 1/2 cups oats
1 1/2 cups sugar
1 cup melted butter or margarine
1 1/2 cups apple butter

In bowl, mix flour, baking soda, and salt. Stir in oats and sugar; mix again. Add butter; blend well. Press half of the mixture firmly into a buttered 9 x 13 x 2 inch baking pan. Spread with apple butter, cover with remaining oat mixture; pat lightly. Bake at 350° F. for 45 to 50 minutes or until lightly browned. Cut into bars. Makes 18-24 bars.

"This recipe is from the collection of Doris Diehl. She is a retired second generation owner of our family business. The third and fourth generations are now working in our orchard and salesroom. This recipe is especially good when you need a different dish to pass. Unsweetened apple butter may be substituted."

Sally Diehl
Diehl's Orchard and Cider Mill
Holly, Michigan

"LEAN" BROWNIES

2 tablespoons applesauce
4 tablespoons oil
1/2 cup egg substitute
1 teaspoon vanilla
1 cup sugar
1/2 cup flour
1/2 teaspoon baking powder
1/2 cup cocoa
1/4 cup chopped nuts

Spray an 8-inch square pan with nonstick cooking spray. Blend together applesauce and oil. Beat in egg substitute and vanilla. Thoroughly beat in sugar. Sift together flour, baking powder, and cocoa. Stir into mixture. Blend in nuts. Bake in preheated 350° F. oven for 35 minutes or until sides start to pull away from pan. Cool in pan on wire rack. Cut into squares. Serves 9.

Each serving: 287 calories, 19 g total fat, 8 g saturated fat, 0 cholesterol

Dorothy Buckingham
Buckingham Orchards
Sunbury, Ohio

APPLE TOFFEE BARS

1 cup plus 2 tablespoons flour
1/2 teaspoon baking powder
1/4 teaspoon baking soda
1/2 teaspoon salt
1/2 cup butter or margarine, softened
1 cup brown sugar, packed
1 teaspoon vanilla
2 eggs
1 cup all-bran cereal
1 cup chopped raw apples, unpeeled
1/4 cup chopped nuts

Sift together flour, baking powder, baking soda, and salt. Cream butter or margarine and brown sugar. Beat in vanilla and eggs. Stir in all-bran cereal. Let stand 2-3 minutes. Add flour mixture. Stir well. Add apples and nuts. Blend in. Pour into greased 9 inch square pan and spread evenly. Bake at 350° F. for 40 minutes. Cool in pan on rack. Cut into bars.

"If desired, bars can be iced with a lemon confectioners' sugar icing."

Dorothy Buckingham
Buckingham Orchards
Sunbury, Ohio

The Ridge Orchards
Bourbon, Missouri

As one might imagine, the work at The Ridge Orchards is invigorating and challenging—but very rewarding. Everyone pitches in to work. Charles Heitsch makes apple cider, and Leona Heitsch dries apples and produces apple leather, apple butter, and apple sauce. Their son, Charles, helps in all aspects of orchard work and also crafts copper and tinware reproductions of early American lighting fixtures.

GAS PEDALS

2 cups flour
1/2 cup sugar
1 cup oatmeal
2 1/2 teaspoons baking powder
1/2 cup canola oil
1 egg
1/2 cup applesauce
1/2 cup black walnuts
1/2 cup raisins
1/2 cup chocolate chips

Combine flour, sugar, oatmeal, baking powder, and oil. Add egg and blend in rest of ingredients. Shape on a greased cookie sheet in flat long strips, with some space in between. Bake at 350° F. for 10 minutes or until done.

"These cookies are so named because, when baked, the strips are cut to form rectangular "gas pedals."

Leona Heitsch
The Ridge Orchards
Bourbon, Missouri

CAKES

The Apple Core Orchard
Durand, Michigan

This poem by Tammy Turner Fox,
daughter of Stan and Marilyn Turner, describes life at:

The Apple Core Orchard

Let's go on a hayride
And then take a walk
An apple for munching
As farmer Stan talks.

You'll learn how the apples
Are raised, picked and sold
While enjoying a donut
With hot cider or cold.

OLD FASHIONED APPLE CAKE

1/2 cup shortening
1 1/2 cups sugar
2 eggs
6 tablespoons buttermilk
2 1/4 cups flour
1 1/2 teaspoons baking soda
1 1/2 teaspoons cinnamon
1 teaspoon nutmeg
3/4 teaspoon salt
3 cups cooking apples, unpeeled, diced

Blend shortening and sugar. Add eggs and buttermilk. Stir in sifted dry ingredients. Add apples last and mix until all ingredients are moistened. Batter will be stiff. Pour into 13 x 9 x 2 inch pan. Bake at 350° F. for 45 minutes.

Caramel/Coconut Frosting
6 tablespoons butter or margarine, melted
2/3 cup brown sugar
1/4 cup cream (or milk)
1/2 teaspoon vanilla
1 cup coconut

Blend butter or margarine, brown sugar, cream or milk, and vanilla together. Spread on cooled cake. Sprinkle coconut on frosting and brown under broiler. Watch carefully.

"This recipe was given to me by my mother-in-law many, many years ago. It is a very old recipe."

Marilyn Turner
The Apple Core Orchard
Durand, Michigan

Emma Krumbee's Restaurant, Apple Orchard, Bakery, Deli, & Country Store

Belle Plaine, Minnesota

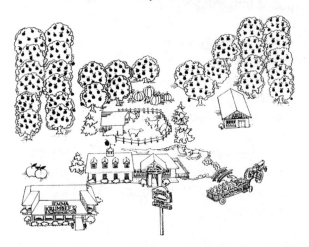

Emma Krumbee's, the star of Apple Country, is much, much more than an apple orchard. The Restaurant, Bakery, Deli, and Country Stores, along with the Apple Orchard, make this a one-stop shopping arena. Set in Belle Plaine, on U.S. Highway 169, less than an hour's drive from Minnesota's Twin Cities, visitors come from all over to enjoy the excellent food, friendly atmosphere, and year around family fun.

From apple blossom time to the Great Scarecrow Festival, Emma Krumbee's is a refreshing escape from the ordinary. You can take the Red Wagon Ride through the apple orchard, stopping by the Animal Farm to visit the friendly farm animals. Or take a nature walk along the beautiful, one-mile orchard path winding through some of Minnesota's most fruitful landscapes.

Emma Krumbee's Restaurant serves a bountiful harvest of delicious breakfasts, lunches, dinners, and desserts all day long. Apple pie is always on the menu, along with many other homemade pies. The dining room and outside deck seating offers a spectacular view of the Apple Orchard.

EMMA'S APPLE CAKE

1 cup sugar
1/2 cup brown sugar
1/2 cup shortening
2 eggs
2 cups flour
1/2 cup buttermilk
2 teaspoons baking soda
1/4 teaspoon salt
2 teaspoons cinnamon
2 cups cut-up raw apple

Beat 1 cup sugar, 1/2 cup brown sugar, 1/2 cup shortening, and 2 eggs with mixer until well mixed. Add flour, buttermilk, baking soda, salt, and cinnamon. Mix until well incorporated. Fold in raw apples. Spread in a greased 9 x 13 inch pan. Sprinkle with topping:

1/4 cup sugar
1/4 cup brown sugar
1 teaspoon cinnamon
1/2 cup walnuts, if desired

Mix 1/4 cup sugar, 1/4 cup brown sugar, 1 teaspoon cinnamon, and walnuts together and sprinkle on top of batter. Bake at 350° F. for 30 to 40 minutes.

Mark Sauter, Head Baker
Emma Krumbees Restaurant, Bakery, Deli, and Apple Orchard
Belle Plaine, Minnesota

The Apple Orchard, Inc.
Harrisonville, Missouri

Bill, Sr. and Sharon Niswonger are relative newcomers to the orchard business, having opened for business on July 4, 1989. Both have full time jobs in Kansas City so orchard hours are limited. Soon they hope to be established on a more full time basis.

The Apple Orchard Inc. is situated in a peaceful setting 5 miles from Harrisonville, Missouri, and one mile west of 71 highway. There is a U-Pick black berry patch in the neighborhood and further down the road is a U-Pick corn patch. Mr. Niswonger says, "This is an excellent area for people to come and find about anything they want in fresh fruit and vegetables and enjoy a nice, fun day in the country."

Pre-picked apples, peaches, tomatoes, green beans, peppers, and other vegetables are offered at the Apple Orchard, Inc. Depending on the crop, some U-Pick may be offered, but they encourage customers to call first.

The store front is situated in a 60 x 100 ft. building where honey, sorghum, cider, jams, and jellies are sold. Apple wood chips for barbecuing are also available, as are crafts that relate to apples or peaches.

About 2000 apple trees are grown, with *Jonathan* being the main variety, along with some *Red* and *Golden Delicious*. Other varieties are now being planted, such as the *Gala* apple. In addition to apples, about 500 peach trees are grown—*Red Haven* being the main variety. Some *Summer Pearls* and *Belle of Georgia* white peaches are also grown.

The Niswongers have taken great care to make their orchard as accessible as possible. For example, the rows are neat and marked with numbers and the grass is kept mowed. Handicap parking is available in front of the store.

An apple processing room and a 22 x 32 ft. walk-in cooler have been added. Since the addition of the cold storage, fruits and vegetables are sold all year around. The Niswongers continue to make improvements that will add to the satisfaction of their customers.

MOM'S APPLE SAUCE CAKE

1/2 cup shortening
1 cup sugar
2 cups sifted flour
1 1/4 teaspoons salt
1 teaspoon baking soda
1/2 teaspoon nutmeg
1 teaspoon cinnamon
1/2 teaspoon cloves
2 cups applesauce
1/2 cup raisins
1/2 cup nuts (pecans or walnuts)

Cream shortening and sugar until light. Sift dry ingredients together and add to the first mixture. Beat in applesauce on low speed of mixer until smooth. Stir in raisins and nuts. Pour into loaf pan (use non-stick pan or line pan with wax paper).

Bake at 325° F. about 1 hour. Let cool slightly, then remove from pan.

Bill and Sharon Niswonger, Sr.
The Apple Orchard, Inc.
Harrisonville, Missouri

Schreiman Orchard
Waverly, Missouri

Travel the 20 mile stretch between Lexington and Waverly and you will see spectacular views of red and golden apples ripening on heavily laden branches. Stop at Schreiman Orchard for a taste of your favorite apples, or try some of the new and different varieties. They have what you want—whether it is a good crisp apple for eating in hand, or a somewhat tart, but firm, apple for all your delicious apple desserts.

Many customers have been coming to the same roadside market for 60 years. Customers tell how they once came by horse and wagon to buy whole loads of Waverly apples to make into cider and apple butter. The soil and terrain gives these apples a flavor all their own.

The on-going theme at Schreiman Orchards is best expressed by Judy Marshall when she says, "We hope you will continue to enjoy the bounty of our country harvest as much as we do growing it for you."

BEST LADIES' AID APPLE CAKE

1 cup shortening
3 cups sugar
4 eggs
Almost 3 cups flour (*see note)
3 tablespoons cornstarch
2 teaspoons baking soda
1/2 teaspoon salt
2 teaspoons nutmeg
2 teaspoons cinnamon
2 cups nuts
6 cups chopped apples

*Note: Measure 2 cups flour then measure 3 tablespoons cornstarch in cup and add enough flour to finish filling cup (total is almost 3 cups flour).

Cream shortening and sugar; add eggs. Sift together dry ingredients. Add to first part. Mix in nuts and chopped apples. Spread batter in greased and floured 9 x 13 inch pan. Bake at 350° F. for 45 minutes.

"It really is a good apple cake and very moist, since it has lots of apples!"

Judy Schreiman Marshall
Schreiman Orchards
Waverly, Missouri

Stark Brothers Nurseries and Orchards Company
Louisiana, Missouri

The Stark family pioneered the development of apples and other orchard stock and they and their firm are recognized today as world leaders in the horticultural field. Through their work, fruit tree knowledge has been vastly expanded in their search for superior strains and plant improvement. As one early Stark founder espoused: "We should raise the best varieties available. It is just as easy to raise a better one like this high quality apple, as it is to raise those poor quality sorts." Stark Brothers Nurseries changed the landscape of America by making it more beautiful and fruitful.

The pioneer James Hart Stark and the five generations who followed him firmly believed that their customers must be provided with every opportunity for successful fruit tree growing. Their orchards would become living testimonials of Stark Trees and Stark service.

Luther Burbank, the plant scientist and one of the greatest mass plant breeders of all time, played an important part in the plant development at the Stark Nurseries. The Stark/Burbank research work in testing new plant varieties and improved methods of propagation and production contributed greatly to the development of better plants. From the time he became associated with the Starks in 1893 until his death in 1926, Mr. Burbank added a wealth of knowledge about fruit growing and left a legacy of rare hybrids, trees, and plants.

APPLE PIE CAKE

1/4 cup butter or margarine, softened
1 cup sugar
1 egg
1 cup flour
1 teaspoon salt
1 teaspoon ground cinnamon
2 tablespoons hot water
1 teaspoon vanilla
3 cups peeled, diced cooking apples
1/2 cup chopped nuts (pecans, walnuts, or black walnuts)

Cream butter or margarine; gradually add sugar and beat at medium speed of mixer until well mixed. Add egg and beat until blended. Combine flour, salt, and cinnamon; mix well. Add to creamed mixture and beat on low speed until smooth. Stir in water and vanilla. Add apples and nuts. Spoon mixture into greased and floured 9 inch pie pan. Bake at 350° F. for 45 minutes or until pick comes out clean when inserted in center of pie. Serve warm or cool with *Rum Butter Sauce* and whipped cream, if desired.

Rum Butter Sauce
1/2 cup brown sugar, packed
1/4 cup butter or margarine, softened
1/2 cup sugar
1 tablespoon rum
1/2 cup whipping cream

Combine first 3 ingredients in small pan; bring to boil over low heat. Cook for one minute. Add rum. Makes 1 1/4 cups. Serve warm or cool over Apple Pie Cake. Whip cream to serve, if desired.

"This Apple Pie Cake won first prize in the 'Apple Anything' contest at the Louisiana, Missouri Country Colorfest in 1987."

Marilyn Johnson
Louisiana, Missouri

GERMAN APPLE CAKE

2 cups sugar
2 cups sifted flour
1 teaspoon baking soda
1/2 teaspoon salt
2 teaspoons cinnamon
1 cup oil
2 eggs
1 cup chopped nuts
4 cups thinly sliced apples
1 cup raisins

In a large bowl, mix together dry ingredients. Add oil and eggs. Beat well with spoon. Do not use mixer. Mix in nuts, apples, and raisins. Batter will be stiff. Spread in greased and floured 9 x 13 inch pan. Bake at 350° F. for 45 minutes or until done. Serve with whipped cream or your favorite vanilla, caramel, or cream cheese frosting.

"This is a very moist cake."

Rose Marie Buchholz
Louisiana, Missouri

COCOA APPLE CAKE

3 eggs
2 cups sugar
1 cup (2 sticks) butter or margarine
1/2 cup water
2 1/2 cups flour
2 tablespoons cocoa
1 teaspoon baking soda
1 teaspoon cinnamon
1 teaspoon allspice
1 cup finely chopped walnuts
1/2 cup chocolate chips
2 cups apples, grated or chopped
1 tablespoon vanilla

Beat together eggs, sugar, butter or margarine, and water until fluffy. Sift together flour, cocoa, baking soda, cinnamon, and allspice. Add to creamed mixture and mix well. Fold in nuts, chocolate chips, apples, and vanilla until evenly distributed. Spoon into greased and floured 10 inch loose bottom tube or angel food cake pan. Bake at 325° F. for 60 to 70 minutes or until cake test done. Yield: 10 servings.

"I use Jonathan or Golden Delicious apples."

June Jennings
Stark Brothers Nursery
Middleton, Missouri

A & M Farm
Midland, Ohio

The A & M Farm has been owned and operated by the Adae family for over fifty years. The fourth generation is now starting to help with the work. The farm has one hundred and eighty acres, most of which is devoted to the raising of fruit. It is located about 45 to 50 minutes east of downtown Cincinnati in beautiful Brown County, Ohio.

Melrose apples, plus many other varieties, are grown. Fresh cider is made without anything added. Orchard services include wagon rides on Saturday and Sunday afternoons in the fall. Large displays of pumpkins are featured in October.

APPLESAUCE CAKE

2 1/2 cups flour
2 cups sugar
1/4 teaspoon baking powder
1 1/2 teaspoons baking soda
1 teaspoon salt
3/4 teaspoon cinnamon
1/2 teaspoon cloves
1/2 teaspoon allspice
1 1/2 cups applesauce
1/2 cup water
1/2 cup shortening
2 eggs
1 cup raisins
1/2 cup finely chopped nuts

Heat oven to 350° F. Grease and flour 9 x 13 x 2 inch pan or 2 round layer pans, 8 or 9 x 1 1/2 inches. Measure all ingredients into large mixer bowl. Blend 1/2 minute on low speed of mixer, scraping bowl constantly. Beat 3 minutes on high speed, scraping bowl occasionally. Pour into pan(s). Bake oblong at 350° F. for 60 - 65 minutes; layers for 50 - 55 minutes or until wooden pick inserted in center comes out clean. Cool.

Alice Adae
A & M Farm
Midland, Ohio

Hillcrest Orchard
Walnut Creek, Ohio

The Hillcrest Orchard is a family operated business owned by Jake and Laura Hershberger. One of their special apples is the old-fashioned *Grimes Golden*. They have their own cider press and cider is a hot item in October each year. Most of the apples are sold retail in their store.

The Hillcrest Orchard was started in 1928. Laura Hershberger's parents bought the 30 acre orchard in 1961 and in 1968 Laura and Jake took over the management. Concerning their business, Laura states: "We all enjoy working together and, in owning a business, we have been privileged to meet many nice, friendly people — our customers."

APPLE CAKE

2 eggs
4 cups diced apples
1/2 cup vegetable oil
1 teaspoon vanilla
2 cups flour
2 cups sugar
2 teaspoons baking soda
1/2 teaspoon salt
1/2 teaspoon cinnamon
1 cup chopped nuts

Break eggs over apples. Stir well. Add vegetable oil. Stir. Mix dry ingredients well and stir into mixture. Pour into 13 x 9 pan and bake at 350° F. for 50- 60 minutes. Make sauce and serve warm over cake.

Sauce
1/4 cup butter
1 cup milk
2 tablespoons flour
3 teaspoons vanilla

Place ingredients in saucepan and cook until thick.

Laura Hershberger
Hillcrest Orchard
Walnut Creek, Ohio

Hollmeyer Orchards
Cincinnati, Ohio

Located 15 miles west of downtown Cincinnati, the Hollmeyer
Orchards grow about 30 varieties of apples. These include *Spy,
Melrose, Mutsu, Ozark Gold, Cortland*, and all of the old standards.

The Hollmeyer Orchards have a long history of being owned by
the same family. William Hollmeyer established the business in 1916.
Before that date it was owned by a cousin.

Vegetables are available through the summer season. "We raise
most everything that we sell in our markets," commented Ron
Hollmeyer.

Hollmeyer Orchards have a reputation for great tasting fresh cider.
They owe the fine rich flavor of their cider to the wide variety of
apples used. Preserves, jellies, and apple butters, with or without
sugar, are also available.

APPLE NUT CAKE

3 eggs
1 3/4 cups sugar
1 cup oil
2 cups flour
1 teaspoon salt
1 teaspoon baking soda
1 teaspoon cinnamon
2 cups peeled and diced apples
(*McIntosh*, good choice)
1 cup chopped nuts

In large bowl, mix eggs, sugar, and oil. Add dry ingredients. Mix well. Stir in apples and nuts. Spread in greased and floured 9 x 13 inch pan. Bake at 350° F. for 45 minutes.

"This cake freezes well."

"Six ounces of butterscotch bits can be added."

Ron Hollmeyer
Hollmeyer Orchards
Cincinnati, Ohio

Gayle Irons
Irons' Fruit Farm
Lebanon, Ohio

Joan B. and David T. Clark
Crow Hill Orchard
St. Johnsbury, Vermont

The Homestead Orchard
Salem, Ohio

James and Mary Kirk have been owners of The Homestead Orchard since 1984. They specialize in personal service to their customers, taking time to visit and help customers with apple selections and educating them about apple varieties and uses. Always encouraging them to "try something new," their customers find many tasty selections at the orchard.

Another interesting highlight of The Homestead Orchard is that Mr. and Mrs. Kirk raise sorghum cane which they press and cook on "Sorghum Saturday." The molasses is then available to customers.

NOBBY APPLE CAKE

1 cup sugar
3 tablespoons butter or margarine
1 egg, beaten
1/2 teaspoon cinnamon
1/2 teaspoon nutmeg
1/2 teaspoon salt
1 teaspoon baking soda
1 cup flour
3 cups diced apples
1/4 cup chopped nuts
1 teaspoon vanilla

Cream sugar and butter or margarine. Add egg and mix well. Mix dry ingredients together and stir into sugar and egg mixture. Stir in vanilla, nuts, and apples. Pour into greased 8 inch square pan. Bake in 350° F. oven for 40 to 45 minutes.

James and Mary Kirk
The Homestead Orchard
Salem, Ohio

Maplewood Orchard
Morrow, Ohio

Maplewood Orchard is a family business owned and operated by Mr. and Mrs. Myron C. Baker. Situated northeast of Cincinnati, the Orchard offers a wide variety of apples from July through the winter. Apple varieties ideal for sauce, such as *Transparent* and *Maiden Blush*, are harvested early. Varieties ideal for pies and desserts, such as *Summer Rambo, Cortland, York*, and *Rome Beauty*, ripen from summer to late fall.

Cider is fresh-squeezed daily from a variety of sound, ripe apples. Ohio Amish cheeses are available and delivered to Maplewood Orchards weekly, along with other Amish products.

APPLESAUCE POUND CAKE

1 (16 oz.) pound cake mix
1 cup unsweetened applesauce
1 egg
1 1/2 teaspoon rum extract

Preheat oven to 350° F. Lightly grease bottom of 9 x 5 x 3 inch loaf pan. Blend pound cake mix, applesauce, egg, and rum extract in bowl. Beat 3 - 4 minutes with electric mixer. Pour into prepared pan. Bake at 350° F. for 65 minutes or until cake is golden brown. Cool 15 minutes before loosening around the edges and removing from pan. Cool completely before serving. Makes 1 loaf.

Dixie A. Baker
Maplewood Orchards
Morrow, Ohio

FRESH-APPLE CAKE

4 cups chopped apples
2 cups sugar
2 eggs
1/2 cup vegetable oil
1 teaspoon vanilla
1 teaspoon salt
2 cups flour
2 teaspoons baking soda
2 teaspoons cinnamon
1 cup nuts
1 cup raisins

Combine apples and sugar; let stand. Beat eggs slightly, beat in oil and vanilla. Sift together flour, baking soda, cinnamon , and salt. Stir in alternately with apple-sugar mixture. Stir in nuts and raisins. Pour into greased and floured 9 x 13 x 2 inch pan. Bake at 350° F. for 45 minutes or until cake tests done.

"May be served plain or frosted with butter or carmel frosting."

Nina Layner
Layner Orchards
Little Hocking, Ohio

Rockwell Orchards
Barnesville, Ohio

Ancestors of the present operators of Rockwell Orchards began growing fruit near Barnesville, Ohio, in the 1850's. James Edgerton was one of several growers in the area who shipped strawberries to cities in the east and midwest, resulting in Barnesville being known as the "strawberry capital of the world." In 1918, James's son, Walter J. Edgerton, purchased the land east of Barnesville, Ohio, where Rockwell Orchards is located, and began growing apples as well as strawberries and raspberries.

Walter Edgerton's oldest daughter, Elizabeth, married Glenn Rockwell in 1930. They expanded the orchard business, acquiring more land, building a cold storage, and planting newer varieties of apples. Two of Glenn and Elizabeth's sons, Louis and Robert, and two grandsons, Jonathan and Jay, are now actively involved in Rockwell Orchards.

Popular varieties include *Mutsu* (a *Yellow Delicious* cross, also called *Crispin*), *Melrose* (the Ohio apple, a *Jonathan* and *Red Delicious* cross), as well as *Gala, Empire,* and *Red* and *Yellow Delicious.*

The sandy soil in which Rockwell's trees are grown gives their apples a distinctive flavor. (Their address is Sandy Ridge Road). Cider, made from a mixture of several varieties of apples, is well-known in the area. Cider-making demonstrations are given during the Ohio Pumpkin Festival in Barnesville, which is held the last week-end in September.

126

ROMAN APPLE CAKE

1 cup sugar
1 1/2 cups flour
1/4 teaspoon salt
1/4 teaspoon baking powder
1 teaspoon baking soda
1/2 cup shortening
1 egg
1/2 cup milk
4 medium apples, grated
1 teaspoon vanilla

Topping
2 tablespoons melted butter
1/2 cup brown sugar
2 teaspoons cinnamon
2 tablespoons flour
1/2 cup chopped nuts

Sift first 5 dry ingredients into mixing bowl. Add shortening, egg, and milk. Mix with mixer on medium speed. Fold in apples and vanilla. Place batter in well-greased and floured 9 inch square pan. Mix topping until crumbly with pastry blender or fork. Sprinkle over top of cake. Bake in 350° F. oven for 45 minutes. Serve warm with ice cream or whipped topping, if desired.

"My mother-in-law, Elizabeth Rockwell, used this recipe when she was featured, at the age of 84, on a local TV program devoted to 'Holiday Recipes'. It was also a favorite of her late husband, Glenn, who was the founder of Rockwell Orchards."

Loisanne Rockwell
Rockwell Orchards
Barnesville, Ohio

Bingham's Orchard and Fruit Market

St. Thomas, Pennsylvania

Bingham's Orchard and Fruit Market has been growing and selling premium quality fruit in the Cumberland Valley since 1928. Robert and Betty Kriner are the third generation, and their son Bill and his wife, Tammy, are the fourth generation to grow fruit on their 200 plus acres of rich mountain soil.

The Kriner's grow cherries, plums, nectarines, peaches, and apples. They sell them by the basket or by the truckload. Apple cider is pressed year around for their market and stores. A free cup of cider is always available. The Market features their own special apple butter, either sweetened or unsweetened spiced, with honey and with sassafras. Special jellies, preserves, and their own canned peaches line their shelves.

APPLE CAKE

3 cups flour
1 teaspoon baking soda
1 teaspoon salt
2 teaspoons cinnamon
2 cups sugar
3 eggs
1 cup oil
3 cups diced apples
1 cup chopped nuts

Sift together dry ingredients in separate bowl. Mix together sugar, eggs, and oil. Add sifted dry ingredients to mixture. Add diced apples and nuts. Grease and flour tube pan. Bake at 350° F. for 1 hour and 20 minutes. Can be baked in 2 large loaf pans at 300° F. for 1 1/2 hours.

"Use less sugar if using sweet apples."

Betty Kriner
Bingham's Orchard
St. Thomas, Pennsylvania

El Vista Orchards, Inc.
Fairfield, Pennsylvania

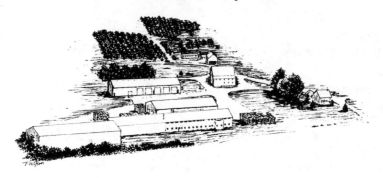

Ten miles west of Gettysburg, Pa., on the slopes of the South Mountains, is the winding spread of El Vista Orchards, Inc. *El Vista* means "the view" in Spanish. And quite a large view, indeed, as over the past 80 years, several farms have been added to the original, with the holdings now totalling over 700 acres.

The history of the El Vista Orchards dates back to the early years of Banks Benner and Elizabeth Musselman, who were married November 28, 1912. In 1915, they moved their household furnishings, automobile, and horse and wagon, to a farm consisting of ninety acres in south central Pennsylvania. The first apple trees were planted in the fall of 1920. As harvests were plentiful, apples were packed in barrels and loaded on railroad cars at a siding located right on the farm.

In 1960 the farms became incorporated with Banks Benner as President and son, Lloyd, as General Manager. Banks died in 1983 and Lloyd in 1984. Today the orchards are operated by Lloyd's widow, Margaret "Peggy" and two sons, David and Jim.

The cold storages have a capacity to hold 100,000 bushels of fruit. This is possible with their combined regular and controlled atmosphere storage, plus a cooler room for storing packed fruit in cartons. Refrigerated trucks are used for shipping.

The El Vista Orchards are both a retail firm and a wholesale business. Sixty percent of the apples are grown for the fresh market trade. Varieties include *Red Delicious, Golden Delicious, Rome Beauty*, plus a few *Empire* and *Gala*. Forty percent of their business crop goes to the wholesale processor.

Kime's Cider Mill
Bendersville, Pennsylvania

While still a junior in high school Robert L. Kime bought his first few acres of land and started growing strawberries and plums. In 1950, he purchased more land and started growing apples and peaches. Then in 1955, Robert purchased a farm in Bendersville, north of Gettysburg, and two year later began pressing fresh apple cider and processing apple butter. Rick and Randy Kime joined their father in partnership in 1977 and the business is now known as Kime's Cider Mill.

APPLE PUDDING CAKE

2 cups sugar
1/2 cup butter
2 eggs
4 cups chopped apples
2 cups flour
2 teaspoons baking soda
1 teaspoon cinnamon
1/4 teaspoon salt
1 teaspoon vanilla
1/2 cup nuts, optional

Cream sugar and butter until light and fluffy. Add eggs and mix well. Add apples. Sift dry ingredients together. Add dry ingredients and vanilla. If desired, nuts can be added. Pour into greased and floured 9 x 13 inch pan. Bake at 350° F. for 1 hour. May be served warm with ice cream or cold with whipped cream.

Peggy Benner
El Vista Orchards, Inc.
Fairfield, Pennsylvania

Donna K. Kime
Kime's Cider Mill
Bendersville, Pennsylvania

Shatzer Fruit Market and Orchards

Chambersburg, Pennsylvania

Located in a fertile valley, Shatzer Orchards has benefitted from its excellent fruit growing locality. Juicy, luscious apple varieties most commonly grown are *Cortland, Stayman, Red* and *Golden Delicious, Yorks, Red Romes*, and *Ida Reds*. Owners Jack, Wilma, and Dwight Mickey have been constant winners at the Franklin County Fair and the Pennsylvania State Farm Show for their fruit exhibits.

Many products are sold at the roadside market, such as apple butter and sweet cider made from their apples, and local honey. Pennsylvania Dutch Hex signs and many books on the Pennsylvania Dutch customs and food are also available.

In the fall, the yard is full of pumpkins on antique bob-sleds. People bring their children and grandchildren from miles around to select a pumpkin from the sleds and have their pictures taken on location. Customers will usually find some member of the family on duty in the market and enjoy this personal contact with the growers.

APPLE CAKE

1 3/4 cups sugar
3 eggs
1 teaspoon vanilla
2 cups flour
1 teaspoon baking soda
1 teaspoon salt
1 teaspoon cinnamon
1 cup cooking oil
1 cup chopped nuts (save 1/2 cup for topping)
5 large apples, sliced fine

Grease and flour a 9 x 13 x 2 inch pan. Mix sugar and eggs until light and fluffy. Add vanilla. Mix flour, baking soda, salt, and cinnamon into egg mixture. Alternate with oil. Fold in apples and nuts. Sprinkle topping over batter before baking. Bake at 375° F. for 45 minutes.

Topping
Mix 1/2 cup nuts with 2 tablespoons brown sugar.

*"A softer apple such as **Cortland** or **McIntosh** is best for this recipe. Have apples at room temperature when peeling and baking the cake so all are at the same temperature when put in the oven."*

Wilma Shatzer Mickey
Shatzer Fruit Market and Orchards
Chambersburg, Pennsylvania

Soergel Orchards
Wexford, Pennsylvania

— SOERGELS ORCHARDS —

CANDRA ANDERSON

Each spring Soergel Orchard hosts a pruning demonstration, a sheep shear, several gardening seminars, and in-door pony rides. In August, they roast sweet corn on weekends and celebrate Digger's birthday. Digger is their 1000 pound pig. They invite all their customers to sing "Happy Birthday," and have ice cream sundaes. All money Digger receives as gifts goes toward "Make-A-Wish" charity.

Mid-September through October, the orchard has activities every weekend for the whole family. Educational tours of the orchard, horse drawn hay rides, a cornstalk maze, craft show, a "Spooky" barn, and cider press demonstrations are a few of the activities. During the week they give field trips for school children. Their gift barn contains unique gifts for the hard-to-buy-for individual. The Garden Center and Greenhouses have beautiful plants and flowers all year around. Pony rides are given and farm animals are near the market for kids to feed and pet. Many birthday parties are scheduled in their party room.

APPLE CAKE

Mix together cinnamon-sugar mixture and set aside:
5 tablespoons sugar
2 teaspoons cinnamon

5 cups apples, peeled and sliced thin

2 cups sugar
1 cup oil
4 eggs
3 cups flour
3 teaspoons baking powder
1/4 cup orange juice
2 1/2 teaspoons vanilla

Cream sugar and oil. Add eggs, one at a time. Add flour and baking powder alternately with orange juice. Add vanilla. Pour into a greased tube pan in layers:
Layer 1: Batter
Layer 2: Apples
Layer 3: Cinnamon-sugar mixture

Bake at 375° F. for 30 minutes, then bake at 350° F. for 1 hour. Total baking time: 1 1/2 hour.

Beth Soergel
Soergel Orchards
Wexford, Pennsylvania

Ski-Hi Fruit Farm

Baraboo, Wisconsin

Of the 325 acres of the Ski-Hi Fruit Farm, about 100 acres support 6,000 apple trees—standard, semi dwarf, and dwarf trees. Since this is an old, established orchard, several old varieties are grown, such as *Duchess, Fameuse, Gem City, Golden Russet, Grimes Golden, Hibernal, McIntosh, Northwestern Greening, Salome, Scott's Winter, Tolman Sweet, Sweet Snow, Wealthy,* and *Wolf River.* Many new varieties are also grown.

CINNAMON-APPLE CAKE

2 eggs
1/2 cup oil
1 teaspoon vanilla
2 cups flour
2 cups sugar
1 teaspoon baking soda
1/4 teaspoon salt
2 teaspoons cinnamon
4 cups chopped apples
1/4 cup nut meats

Topping
1/2 cup brown sugar
1 teaspoon cinnamon
1/2 cup chopped nuts

Beat eggs, oil, and vanilla. Add sifted ingredients. Mix well. Add apples and nuts. Pour into greased and floured 9 x 13 inch pan. Mix the topping and sprinkle on top of the batter. Bake at 350° F. for 35-45 minutes.

Olga Marie Bassett
Ski-Hi Fruit Farm
Baraboo, Wisconsin

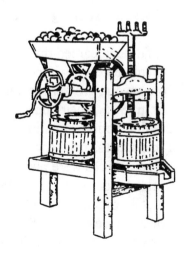

137

Fleming Orchards
Gays Mills, Wisconsin

Gays Mills is the home of a large number of apple orchards, including Fleming Orchards. Steep hills with breathe taking views of valleys surround the visitor on every side in this unglaciated area of Wisconsin. Rock outcroppings have been estimated to be millions of years old.

Early on, farmers learned that both sides of the Kickapoo River offered excellent apple-growing conditions. Apple samples were collected from several growers around Gays Mills for the exhibition at the State Fair in 1905. Their apple exhibition won first place and went on to capture first honors at national competition in New York. Because of this success, trial orchards were set up around the state. Five acres of apple trees were planted on High Ridge, also known as Little Switzerland, near Gays Mills. In a few years they produced so abundantly that an organization was formed to promote the selling of orchards. Today, more than 2,000 acres are devoted to apple growing by various growers in the Gays Mills area.

APPLESAUCE CAKE

1/2 cup butter or margarine
1 cup sugar
2 eggs
1 1/2 cups sweetened applesauce
2 teaspoons baking soda
1 1/2 cups flour
1 1/2 cups raisins
Nuts, if desired

Cream butter or margarine; add sugar and eggs. Beat well. Add applesauce. Combine baking soda, flour, raisins, and nuts; add to mixture. Bake at 350° F. for 30 to 35 minutes in a greased 9 x 13 inch pan. Cool and frost.

Caramel Frosting
1 cup brown sugar
2 tablespoons butter
3 tablespoons Crisco™
1/4 cup milk
1 cup confectioners' sugar

Combine first 4 ingredients in medium saucepan and boil for three minutes. Cool and add 1 cup confectioners' sugar. Mix until smooth and right consistency.

Ruth M. Fleming
Fleming Orchards
Gays Mills, Wisconsin

TOPPINGS FOR APPLE CAKES

Lemon Sauce

1/2 cup sugar
1/4 cup cornstarch
1 cup water
2 tablespoons butter or margarine
2 tablespoons lemon juice
1/2 teaspoon grated lemon rind
Few drops yellow food coloring, optional

Mix together sugar and cornstarch in small saucepan. Gradually stir in water and place over medium heat. Cook until mixture boils and thickens, stirring constantly. Remove from heat and add butter, lemon juice, and rind. Add few drops yellow food coloring. Serve warm over baked cake.

Caramel Topping

1/2 cup brown sugar
1 tablespoon cornstarch
1 cup apple cider or apple juice
3 tablespoons butter or margarine
1 teaspoon vanilla

In saucepan, blend cornstarch with brown sugar. Add cider or juice. Cook over medium heat until thick and clear. Remove from heat; add butter and vanilla. Serve over baked cake.

Cream Cheese Frosting

3 oz. Neufchatel, or light cream cheese
2 cups confectioners' sugar, sifted
1 teaspoon vanilla

Soften Neufchatel or cream cheese. Slowly stir in sugar until of spreading consistency. Add vanilla and a little milk, if necessary.

PIES AND
PASTRY

Lyman Orchards
Middlefield, Connecticut

Lyman Orchards have resided within one family's stewardship for over 250 years. With the initial purchase of 36 acres in 1741 by John Lyman (1717-1763) great, great grandson of Richard Lyman, who set foot ashore in 1631, the farm's fortunes have waxed and waned for eight generations. Through good times and bad the land has been both anchor and inspiration for a wide variety of activities besides farming. These activities have ranged from the manufacture of clothes wringers, gunsights, and reloading tools, to building a railroad, and, more recently, constructing an 18-hole golf course. The changes at the farm paralleled the changing faces of America.

Lyman Orchards is about equal distant from Hartford, New Haven, and Waterbury, Connecticut. The original tract has grown to many hundreds of acres.

The Lyman family forebears were both industrious and colorful. William (1783-1869) was an outspoken abolitionist and rumored to have been part of the "underground railway" that harbored runaway slaves. His son, David (1820-1871) father of nine, built the present homestead, manufactured clothes wringers, and was prime builder of the "Airline" railroad whose purpose was to provide a shorter link between New York and Boston. His brother, Will was inventor of the metallic "peepsight" which gave birth to the Lyman Gunsight Corporation. Lyman Gunsights are still being manufactured in Middlefield.

David's son, Charles Elihu (1857-1923), introduced crop specialization and brought the farm to its zenith in size and production by growing 800 acres of peaches, fattening thousands of lambs for spring sale, and harvesting tons of timothy hay for horse feed and packing material. Before commerical refrigeration, Connecticut was the "peach state" by reason of its proximity to major centers of population. To pick, pack, and ship to market within a 48-hour period were the demands of a successful peach operation. A disastrous winter freeze in 1917-18 destroyed most of the thousands of trees, ending one of the state's most colorful industries. Never again was agriculture to hold such prominence in the state's economy. The hardier apple is now the farm's major crop, with lesser crops of peaches, pears, and small fruits. The farm's large herd of purebred Guernsey dairy cattle was phased out in the mid-60's, leaving many unused acres. This paved the way for Lyman Orchards golf course, which opened to the public in 1969.

Ever since it opened in 1972 to meet the demand for fresh, farm-grown fruit, Lyman Orchards Farm Store has merged into and become part of the beautiful Connecticut countryside. From the warm days of April until early November, this unique circular store expands with a colorful striped tent to add an open-air farmers' market. The area becomes loaded with the freshest fruit and vegetables from their own acres, their freshly pressed cider, and other native produce in season. During winter and early spring, holiday greens and decorative bedding plants are available.

The store's farm kitchen bakery produces breads, pies, muffins, and cookies throughout the week. A complete deli offers sharp cheeses, fresh salads, and take-out foods. Several lines of specialty foods help round out the abundance of the store.

The Lyman Orchards Farm Store is the focal point for a variety of family-oriented events. There are activities such as an old-fashioned maple syrup on snow winterfest, the Easter Apple Hunt, blossom-time and drive-through tours, strawberry jamborees, craft shows, peach or corn festivals, harvest days and fair days, art shows, apple pie baking contests, holidays fests, and Santa. " Going to Lymans" is an often repeated phrase in Connecticut.

APPLE PIE

Crust
2 cups flour
(1 cup white, 1 cup whole wheat)
1 teaspoon salt
2/3 cup shortening
5-7 tablespoons cold water

Filling
6-7 large apples, peeled, cored, and sliced
1 cup sugar
1 teaspoon cinnamon
2 tablespoons flour
Dash nutmeg
1 tablespoon butter

Toss apples with sugar and cinnamon mixture. Set aside.

To prepare crust, mix flour and salt. Cut in shortening, 1/3 cup at a time. Using fork, lightly mix in water, a tablespoon at a time. Form into a ball. Divide dough in half. Roll first half and line pie tin. Fill with apple mixture. Dot with butter. Using knife, cut edge of bottom crust to fit pie tin. Roll top crust carefully from center out. This top crust can be poked with fork holes and should be cut 1/4 to 1/2 inch larger than bottom crust when filled with the apple mixture. Place over apples and tuck under edges; flute crust. Bake in preheated 425° F. oven for 15 minutes, then turn oven down to 325° F. and bake for 45 minutes more. Serve with cheddar cheese.

This recipe was a winner in the apple pie baking contest held at Lyman Orchards.

Lyman Orchards
Middlefield, Connecticut

Bob's Bluebird Orchard and Craft Barn

Webster, Minnesota

In 1994, a craft barn was added to Bob's Bluebird Orchard. The Craft Barn features a wide variety of handmade items by regional artisans. Gift baskets are prepared at the orchard with their apples, other food products, dried flowers, and craft items.

PRAIRIE SPY PASTRY

Pastry for a two-crust pie

4 medium *Prairie Spy* apples
1/3 cup brown sugar
1 teaspoon cinnamon
4 teaspoons butter
1/4 cup raisins

Roll out pastry as for pie and cut in 7 to 8 inch squares. Peel and core apples, but leave whole. Place an apple on each square of dough and fill cavity with mixture of sugar, raisins, cinnamon, and butter. Bring opposite points of dough up to overlap apple. Moisten to seal. Place in baking dish. Bake at 400° F. for 40-45 minutes, or until apples are done and pastry is brown. If desired, serve with warm syrup or ice cream.

Bob and Linda Leis
Bob's Bluebird Orchard
Webster, Minnesota

Louisburg Cider Mill
Louisburg, Kansas

Tom and Shelly Schierman added several product lines, including their immensely popular Lost Trail Root Beer to complement their original fresh apple cider. There is a special window to view the **Juice Works**, which is the bottling and processing plant for all their products. Fresh donuts are served with their cider. The Louisburg Cider Mill is dedicated to producing food and gifts that reflect the marvelous bounty of the land of Kansas.

APPLE CIDER PIE

Pastry for a one-crust 9-inch pie

2 cups sliced *Jonathan* apples
1 tablespoon lemon juice
1/2 cup sugar
3 eggs
1 cup heavy cream
1/4 cup Louisburg Apple Cider
1/4 teaspoon cinnamon
1/4 teaspoon nutmeg
2 tablespoons sugar

Preheat oven to 400° F. Fit pastry into a 9-inch pan. Toss apple slices with lemon juice and 1/2 cup of sugar. Arrange apples in pie crust. Bake at 400° F. for 10 minutes. Reduce heat to 350° F.; bake 20 minutes more. Beat eggs slightly in a bowl. Stir in cream, apple cider, and spices. Pour over apples. Bake 15 minutes more. Sprinkle with remaining 2 tablespoons sugar. Bake 15 minutes more until top is golden. Cool for 2 hours before cutting.

"Try using apple cider for the liquid in muffins, biscuits, breads, rolls, pancakes, and waffles."

Rachelle Schierman
Louisburg Cider Mill, Inc.
Louisburg, Kansas

Coon Creek Orchard
Armada, Michigan

Coon Creek Orchard's logo is "We're still Country." Their
customers come to enjoy the great outdoors, as well as to choose
from among the riches of the harvest.

While munching on freshly made apple cinnamon donuts and
enjoying a freshly pressed cup of apple cider, customers may find that
turkeys, geese, ducks, and chickens will try to steal their food. But not
to worry! Donuts stolen by the animals will be replaced at no charge.
Heidi the cow, Michelle and Marcus the goats, and Helga and Klaus
the sheep, as well as their offspring, will be watching intensely from
their pasture. The barn yard kittens and the young peacock family will
do their best to gain the attention of customers.

Picnic areas by the pond, stream, new orchard, and by the cider
mill are available to all customers to enjoy. Group tours, school
outings, evening hay rides with bon fires, and barn rental are available
upon reservation.

FRENCH APPLE PIE

Make your own pastry or use one frozen pie crust

Pie Filling

For 9-inch pie
3/4 to 1 cup sugar
1 teaspoon cinnamon
   or nutmeg
6-7 cups sliced pared apples
1 1/2 tablespoons butter

For 8-inch pie
1/2 to 3/4 cup sugar
3/4 teaspoon
cinnamon or nutmeg
4-5 cups sliced pared
   apples
1 tablespoon butter

Mix sugar and cinnamon. Mix lightly through apples. Heap up in pastry lined pie pan. Dot with butter. Sprinkle with following crumb topping.

Crumb Topping

For 9-inch pie
1/2 cup butter
1/2 cup brown sugar
1 cup flour

For 8-inch pie
1/3 cup butter
1/3 cup brown sugar
3/4 cup flour

Mix all ingredients until crumbly. Bake at 400° F. for 45 to 55 minutes.

Delores Brown
Coon Creek Orchard
Armada, Michigan

Diehl's Orchard and Cider Mill
Holly, Michigan

Diehl's Orchard grows apples and plums on 75 acres. The business has evolved into a seasonal market with entertainment on fall weekends. Weather permitting, pony and hay rides are given on those weekends. A large pumpkin patch is available at Halloween. For the holidays, they ship apples anywhere in the continental U.S.A.

DIEHL'S APPLE PIE

5 large Diehl's apples
3/4 cup sugar
2 tablespoons flour
Dash nutmeg
1 teaspoon cinnamon
1/8 teaspoon salt
2 tablespoons butter
2 - 9-inch unbaked pie crusts

Peel and core Diehl's apples. Slice thin and combine with sugar, flour, spices, and salt. Fill pie shell with apple mixture and dot with butter. Put on top crust and slit for steam. Bake at 400° F. for 15 minutes and 25 minutes at 350° F. or until done.

Perfect Pie Crust

4 cups flour
1 3/4 cups vegetable shortening
1 tablespoon sugar
2 teaspoons salt
1 tablespoon vinegar
1 egg
1/2 cup cold water

With a fork, mix together the first four ingredients. In a separate dish, beat remaining ingredients. Combine the two mixtures, stirring with a fork until all ingredients are moistened. With hands, mold dough into a ball. Chill at least 30 minutes before rolling out. Dough can be refrigerated up to 3 days or can be frozen up to 3 months. Makes three double crust 9-inch pies or six 9-inch shells.

This recipe is reprinted with permission from Diehl's information flyer given out at the Orchard every fall.

Sally Diehl
Diehl's Orchards and Cider Mill
Holly, Michigan

Morton Orchard at Arbor Day Farm

Nebraska City, Nebraska

Morton Orchard at Arbor Day Farm is owned and operated by **The National Arbor Day Foundation** which is a non-profit educational organization dedicated to promoting tree planting and conservation throughout the United States.

Morton Orchard has a rich history, having once been part of Arbor Day founder J. Sterling Morton's estate. It was J. Sterling and Caroline Morton's oldest son, Joy, who planted the first commercial orchard in Nebraska City in the early 1920's. In 1925, Joy Morton and his partner, Grove Porter, began the Joy Morton Orchard Company, the largest single orchard planting in the Midwest. They planted 160 acres of apples and Montmorency cherries. During the 1930's, thousands of bushels of apples were shipped from Nebraska City in iced railroad cars as far away as Chicago and Denver.

In 1940, Grove Porter became the sole owner of the orchard when he purchased Joy Morton's interest in the farm after Joy's death. He renamed it Porter Orchard and managed the property as a family business until 1975 when he sold the orchard and surrounding farmland to **The National Arbor Day Foundation**. Grove Porter's son, Mort, is the orchard manager and horticulturist for the orchard today.

Morton Orchard at Arbor Day Farm is located in the Missouri River Valley. The rich loess soil is perfect for growing apples. Four major varieties of apples are grown: *Jonathan, Red Delicious, Golden Delicious*, and *Winesap*.

Visitors to Arbor Day Farm can tour the Orchard/Apple House, learn about the antique apple varieties grown in the Preservation Orchard, and hike the Mitchell D. Ferrill Tree Trail. They can also marvel at the magnificent **Lied Conference Center**—the only facility of its kind in the nation with staff and programs dedicated to tree planting and conservation.

APPLE PIE A'PLENTY

Filling
8 cups sliced apples
2 - 2 1/2 cups sugar
1/4 cup flour
1 tablespoon cinnamon

Topping
1 1/2 cups flour
2/3 cups sugar
12 tablespoons butter or margarine

Make pastry for a double crust pie. Pat pastry into a 9 x 13 inch pan, forming and crimping edges as usual. Peel and thinly slice enough apples (about 8 cups) to fill pastry lined pan. Combine apples with sugar, flour, and cinnamon. Place this apple filling mixture in pan and sprinkle with topping. Bake at 375° F. for 1 hour or until done. Number of servings: 15-18.

Mary Porter
Morton Orchard at Arbor Day Farm
Nebraska City, Nebraska

Irons' Fruit Farm
Lebanon, Ohio

Capture the spirit of the season at Irons' Fruit Farm. In addition to their many varieties of apples, a farm bakery is operated June through December. Cider donuts, apple pies, fritters, dumplings, and turnovers are featured in September and October. Apple cider is made September through February. Apple butter, jams, and jellies are also made and holiday fruit/gift baskets and boxes are offered. Fall is the busiest time, with many school groups coming for orchard tours and hayrides and to choose just the right pumpkin. A variety of animals, including white-tail deer, are enjoyed by all.

APPLE PIE IN SQUARES

Crust
2 1/2 cups flour
2 tablespoons sugar
1 teaspoon salt
1 cup shortening
1 egg, beaten
1/3 cup milk (see recipe directions)

Filling
2/3 cup corn flakes, crushed
5 cups sliced apples
1 1/2 cups sugar (less for sweet apples)
1 1/2 teaspoons cinnamon
1 beaten egg (or egg white)

Glaze
1 cup confectioners' sugar
2 tablespoons lemon juice

Blend 2 1/2 cups flour, 2 tablespoons sugar, and 1 tablespoon salt. Cut in 1 cup shortening. Beat 1 egg and add milk to make 2/3 cup. Add to flour mixture and stir with fork. Divide dough in half and roll out 11 x 15 inches. Place 1 layer on cookie sheet.

For filling, sprinkle 2/3 cup crushed corn flakes over dough. Mix apples, sugar, and cinnamon, then arrange over corn flakes. Roll out top layer of dough and place over apples. Beat 1 egg and brush over crust. Bake at 350° F. for 35-40 minutes, until golden brown. Mix confectioners' sugar and lemon juice; drizzle glaze over warm pie. Cut in squares and serve warm. Add vanilla ice cream, if desired.

"We have served this to our farm market customers during the holiday season and also for family gatherings."

Gayle Irons
Irons' Fruit Farm
Lebanon, Ohio

Masonic Homes Orchard
Elizabethtown, Pennsylvania

Since the Masonic Homes Orchard produces more fruit than it needs for its residents, the apples, cider and other apple products are sold through a retail sales operation and mail order business. In this way they can share their gifts with others. Noted for their apple butters that are sweetend with white grape juice (no sugar added), their products continue to be held in high regard and savored by young and old alike.

TOPSY TURVY APPLE PIE

Glaze
1/4 cup brown sugar, packed
1 tablespoon butter, melted
1 tablespoon corn syrup
1/4 cup pecan halves

Pastry for 2 crust pie

Filling
2/3 cup sugar
2 tablespoons flour
1/4 teaspoon cinnamon
4 cups sliced, peeled apples

In a 9 inch pie pan, combine brown sugar, butter, and corn syrup; mix well. Spread mixture evenly in bottom of pan; arrange pecans over mixture. Prepare pastry for 2 crust pie. Place bottom pastry over mixture in pan, gently pressing pastry to fit pan. Heat oven to 425° F.

In small bowl, combine sugar, flour, and cinnamon; mix well. Arrange half of apple slices in pastry lined pan. Sprinkle with half of sugar mixture. Repeat with remaining apple slices and sugar mixture. Top with remaining pastry. Fold edge of top pastry under bottom pastry. Press together to seal and flute edge. Cut slits in several places in top pastry. Bake at 425° F. for 8 minutes. Reduce oven temperature to 325° F.; bake 25-35 minutes, until apples are tender. Remove and carefully invert onto serving plate.

Tad E. Kuntz
Masonic Homes Orchard
Elizabethtown, Pennsylvania

R & R Orchards
Myerstown, Pennsylvania

Ray and Ruth Dundore grow mainly nectarines in their orchard but many apple varieties are also available such as *Jonathan, JonGold, Red* and *Yellow Delicious, Granny Smith, Winter Banana, Idared,* and *Empire.* Mr. Dundore has a unique method of propping up fruit-laden branches. He finds that cast-off crutches work just fine to hold up the heavy fruit-laden branches in the orchard. He said that the propped up limping limbs get a lot of attention!

APPLE PIE IN A BAG

2 1/2 pounds baking apples (3 or 4)
1 cup sugar
1/2 cup + 2 tablespoons flour
1/2 teaspoon cinnamon
1/2 cup soft butter or margarine
Lemon juice
Large brown paper bag

Unbaked 9 inch pie shell

Prepare favorite pastry or packaged pie crust mix and fit into deep 9 inch pie pan. Heat oven to 400° F.

Wash, pare, and quarter apples; cut each quarter into 4 pieces. In large bowl, toss apple chunks with mixture of 1/2 cup sugar, 2 tablespoons flour, and cinnamon until all pieces are coated. Fill pie shell, piling high in center. Sprinkle with lemon juice. Thoroughly mix 1/2 cup each of sugar and flour and butter into a soft paste; spread over top of pie. Place pie in paper bag and close end. Set on rack in center of oven and bake at 400° F. for about 1 hour or until pie is done and nicely browned. Remove from oven — let cool 5 to 10 minutes before carefully removing it from bag.

Ruth Dundore
R & R Orchard
Myerstown, Pennsylvania

The Apple Barn
Bennington, Vermont

Southern Vermont orchards in Bennington, Vermont was
originally established by Edward Hamlin Everett. Born in Cleveland,
Ohio in 1852, Everett lived his boyhood years in Bennington. As a
young man, he left Vermont and soon became involved in the
industrial growth of the late 1800's. In 1910 he returned to
Bennington to live—by then he was a wealthy and influential man.

In the spring of 1912, Mr. Everett began setting out apple trees.
By 1920, he had extended his holdings over ten miles. On this land he
planted cherries, quince, pears, and plums, as well as 65 varieties of
apples. Under his guidance, Everett Orchards became one of the
largest privately owned orchards in the world, renowned for its
modern agricultural practices and high quality fruit.

Following Everett's death in 1929, his property was gradually
divided and sold. Today Southern Vermont Orchards is owned by
Harold Albinder, who operates all the original orchard that remains in
production.

Located on Carpenter Hill, over 300 acres of orchard continue to
benefit from Everett's wise selection of location which enables the
orchard to continue to raise an apple of unique quality. Groups are
invited to stop by and enjoy the beauty of Carpenter Hill and the
Vermont hillside, as well as the delicious apples. Varieties grown
include *Red* and *Golden Delicious, Macoun, Mutsu, Northern Spy,
McIntosh, Cortland, Empire, Idared* and others.

At the Sales Barn, visitors will find apples, cider, cheese, fresh
produce, pumpkins, preserves, Vermont maple products, and dried
flowers. Their Country Bakery has over 20 varieties of pies, tarts,
brownies, cookies, tea breads, muffins, breads, and other bakery
products. They invite you to take a taste of Southern Vermont for
quality products from the heart of Southern Vermont Orchards.

BUMBLEBERRY PIE

3 cups raspberries
3 cups blackberries
3 cups strawberries
3 cups blueberries
3 cups rhubarb
3 cups thinly sliced apples
1 cup sugar
1 cup flour

4 - 9-inch pie shells

Mix together all ingredients. Put into pie shells and cover with dough top or crumb top. Bake at 350º F. for 50 to 60 minutes.

Harry Diamond
The Apple Barn of Southern Vermont Orchards
Bennington, Vermont

NO SUGAR APPLE PIE

1 - 9 inch pie shell

1 1/2 pounds sliced apples
1/4 cup apple cider
1 tablespoon cinnamon

Mix apples, cider, and cinnamon. Put into pie shell. Cover with dough top. Brush on an egg glaze (1 egg beaten with 2 teaspoons of water). Bake at 350° F. for 50 to 60 minutes or until apples are tender.

Harry Diamond
The Apple Barn of Southern Vermont Orchards
Bennington, Vermont

Countryside Apple Center
Kenosha, Wisconsin

Carl and Mike Bullmore are the original owners of Countryside Apple Center, which was established in 1979. They started with 25 trees for family use and enjoyment. Now they have 1250 trees serving two farmers' markets and local retail. Being close to Lake Michigan helps to give them their good growing conditions.

OLD WORLD OPEN FACE APPLE PIE

Standard recipe for one-crust 9-inch pie

3 to 5 apples, sliced 1/4 inch thick,
peeled or unpeeled
(*Red* or *Yellow Delicious* or *Gala* is a good choice)
Lemon juice
3 tablespoons sugar
Apricot jam

Toss sliced apples in lemon juice. Roll out pie crust and fit into 9 inch or larger pie plate. Cover with apples in circular design — overlapping slightly. Dust top with sugar. Bake 30 minutes at 425° F. Remove and dust with sugar again. Melt apricot jam over medium heat and brush glaze on apples. Garnish with fresh thyme. Makes 6 servings.

Carl Bullmore
Countryside Apple Center
Kenosha, Wisconsin

Waqua Farm Orchard
Rawlings, Virginia

Waqua Farm Orchard was the home place of Eddria Allene Coleman Fisher, one of the present co-owners. Her parents raised eight children on this farm. Their primary cash crop was tobacco. The family sustained themselves almost entirely on the produce they raised — garden crops, chickens, and hogs. The corn and wheat were taken to the local mill to be ground for meal and flour.

Back then, the family planted and maintained about thirty fruit trees, as well as grape vines. It was this tradition of the family orchard that the current owners, the Richard and Daniel Fisher families wanted to continue, although on an expanded scale. Since 1985 they have planted 400-600 fruit trees each year. Their "home orchard" has expanded to approximately 20 acres. For them, the Farm Orchard is not only a business enterprise, it is also their home.

About thirty varieties of apples are available at Waqua Farm Orchard. All of their apples are semi-dwarf, growing only 10-12 feet tall, so no more than a 2-step ladder is required to pick. Apple cider is made by hand on an old fashioned cider press. They have a nice pond with ducks and geese, and also a sheltered picnic area with a barbecue.

EASY APPLE PIE

1 deep dish 9 inch pie crust

4 large apples
(*Arkansas Black* is a good choice)
1/2 cup sugar
1 teaspoon cinnamon
1/2 cup sugar
3/4 cup flour
1/3 cup butter

Peel apples, core, and slice. Sprinkle with 1/2 cup sugar and cinnamon. Put apples in pie crust. Mix remaining sugar and flour together. Cut in butter, and sprinkle mixture over top of apples. Bake at 450° F. for 10 minutes, then at 350° F. for about 40 minutes.

Sharon Fisher
Waqua Farm Orchard
Rawlings, Virginia

Ski-Hi Fruit Farm
Baraboo, Wisconsin

Olga Marie Bassett of Ski-Hi Fruit Farm shares the following information about early apple varieties, many with a Wisconsin connection:

"The apple variety, *Gem City*, was a seedling discovered in Wisconsin before 1905 and grown in Baraboo, Wisconsin. *Duchess* and *Wealthy* were recommended on the apple list in 1889. *Hibernal* is a Russian variety used mostly for root stock because it tolerates severe winters. *McIntosh* is another seedling discovered on a farm in Ontario, Canada and was introduced to the USA in 1907. *Northwestern Greening* was a seedling originated near Iola, Wisconsin and introduced in 1872. It is favored by processors for its uniform size and for canning as well as for freezing. *Wolf River* is another seedling found near the village of Freemont, Wisconsin and the Wolf River, hence its name. It was first mentioned in 1875."

SURPRISE APPLE TWISTS

Crust
1/4 cup butter
1/4 cup sour cream
1/2 cup flour

Filling
5 apples, pared and cut in wedges
2 tablespoons flour
1/2 cup sugar
1/4 teaspoon cinnamon
1/4 teaspoon nutmeg

Frosting
1 1/2 cups confectioners' sugar
2 teaspoons milk
1 teaspoon vanilla
1/2 cup chopped hickory nuts

In bowl, beat softened butter and sour cream until fluffy. Add flour and mix well. Cover and chill for 1 hour until firm enough to handle. Roll into 10 x 8 inch rectangle; place on greased 9 x 13 inch pan.

In bowl, mix flour, sugar, and spices; add apples and coat well. Spread apples through center of rectangle of pastry. Make cuts 2 1/2 inches deep at one-inch intervals along both sides. Fold strips over filling; pinching into narrow points at center. Bake at 350° F. for 30 minute or until done. Make frosting and drizzle over twist. Sprinkle hickory nuts over pastry.
"Hickory nuts are native to Wisconsin."

Olga Marie Bassett
Ski-Hi Fruit Farm
Baraboo, Wisconsin

APPLE ROSETTES

Crust
1 cup flour
1/4 teaspoon salt
1/3 cup Crisco™
3 tablespoons cold water

4 medim apples, pared and cored
1/2 cup sugar
1 tablespoon flour
1/4 teaspoon nutmeg
1/4 teaspoon cinnamon
1 tablespoon butter, cut in chunks

In mixing bowl, mix flour, salt, and Crisco ™ to form crumbs.
Add cold water to form a ball. Roll on floured pastry cloth into a
rectangle. Cut into long strips one-inch wide to wrap around apples.
Starting from bottom, wind around apple to the top. Put apples into
greased 8 x 8 inch pan.

Mix together sugar, flour, nutmeg, and cinnamon. Spoon sugar
mixture into center of apples and put a dab of butter on top of each
rosette. Bake at 400° F. oven for 30 minutes or until apples are done.
Serve with scoop of ice cream.

Olga Marie Bassett
Ski-Hi Fruit Farm
Baraboo, Wisconsin

Glennie Orchard
New Berlin, Wisconsin

Glennie Orchard is located in the Wisconsin apple country of New Berlin. Donavan Glennie and his wife, Elanor bought the orchard in 1978.

There are about 25 varieties of apples grown at the Glennie Orchard. These include many new as well as older varieties. Some of the apple trees date back to 1935. Of the many varieties of apples grown, Mrs. Glennie likes the *Jonathan* because of its tart taste and versatility.

For best results in home storage, Mrs. Glennie suggests putting apples in a plastic bag with pre-punched holes and storing them in a crisper in the refrigerator. This way, they stay firm and juicy, ready to be eaten in hand or used in any of your favorite dishes. The following are two pie recipes from Elanor Glennie's cookbook of wonderful apple treats.

GLENNIE ORCHARD DUTCH APPLE PIE

For the struesel top, combine:
1 1/3 cups flour
1/2 cup sugar
1/2 cup melted butter or margarine

Mix together with a fork until crumbly. Refrigerate for 1/2 hour.

For the no-roll crust, combine with a fork:
1 1/2 cups flour
2 teaspoons sugar
1 teaspoon salt
1/2 cup oil
2 tablespoons milk

Divide in half and press into two 7-inch pie pans.

Peel and slice approximately 10 to 12 medium baking apples and place on top of the crusts slightly mounded. Sprinkle each with:
1/2 teaspoon cinnamon
2 tablespoons sugar
1/4 teaspoon nutmeg, optional
Dot with 1/2 tablespoon butter

Cover all apples with the streusel mixture. Cover with tin foil. Bake in pre-heated 425° F. oven for 20 minutes. Reduce oven to 350° F. and bake for another 50 minutes. Remove the tin foil for the last 20 minutes to brown the streusel. Cool.

Elanor Glennie
Glennie Orchard
New Berlin, Wisconsin

APPLE PASTRY BARS

8-10 apples, peeled and sliced
1 cup sugar
1 teaspoon cinnamon
1 teaspoon salt
1 cup cornflake crumbs

Crust
2 1/2 cups flour
2 tablespoons sugar
1 cup shortening
1/2 teaspoon salt
2 eggs
Milk

Peel apples and mix in sugar, cinnamon, and salt. Set aside.

In bowl, mix together dry ingredients and cut in shortening. Separate eggs and beat egg yolks in cup. Add milk to make 2/3 cup liquid. Add egg/milk mixture and lightly stir in with fork. Form it into a ball. Divide in half and roll one-half to fit 9 x 13 inch pan. Spread 1 cup cornflake crumbs over pastry. Add apple mixture. Roll out rest of dough and put over apples. Seal edges and make slits in crust. Beat egg whites slightly and spread over top. Bake at 350° F. for 40 minutes. Test to see if apples are done. Powdered sugar icing can be drizzled over the top.

Elanor Glennie
Glennie Orchard
New Berlin, Wisconsin

Krueger's Orchard
Godfrey, Illinois

Paul and Jo Ann Krueger started their family-owned and operated business in 1976. Over the next two years, they planted more fruit trees until, as Mrs. Krueger pointed out, "Our ground was filled!"

KRUEGER'S APPLE DUMPLINGS

Prepare your favorite pie crust recipe. Separate dough in either two or three sections. Roll out dough in oblong form rather than in a circle.

Peel, core, and slice apples and spread on pie crust in a couple of layers. Roll crust and apples in jelly roll fashion. Pinch edges together and slice in 1/2 to 3/4 inch slices. Place in greased cake pan with cut sides down. Repeat with rest of pie crust. Bake in 350° F. oven about 30 to 35 minutes or until apples are fork tender. As soon as this is done baking, have *Cinnamon Sauce Syrup* ready and pour over dumplings. Serve warm or cold.

Cinnamon Sauce Syrup
2 cups sugar
2 cups water
1/2 teaspoon cinnamon
3 tablespoons flour
1 teaspoon vanilla
1 tablespoon butter or margarine

Combine first five ingredients in saucepan. Bring to boil. Remove from heat and add butter or margarine.

Jo Ann Krueger
Krueger's Orchard
Godfrey, Illinois

Schweizer Orchard
Amazonia, Missouri

Savor the scenic views near the bluffs of the Missouri River and taste the goodness of the fruit at Schweizer Orchard. Both of their retail locations can be easily reached from Interstate 29 in northern Missouri.

SCHWEIZER'S APPLE DUMPLINGS

Pastry for 9 inch two-crust pie

6 medium tart apples
1 cup sugar
2 cups water
3 tablespoons butter
1/4 teaspoon cinnamon
1/2 cup sugar
1 1/2 teaspoons cinnamon
1 tablespoon butter

Heat oven to 425° F. Roll out pastry a little less than 1/8 inch thick and cut into six 7-inch squares. Pare and core apple for each dumpling.

Boil next 4 ingredients together for 3 minutes to make hot syrup.

Place apple on each square of pastry. Fill cavities of apples with mixture of 1/2 cup sugar and 1 1/2 teaspoons cinnamon. Dot each with butter. Bring opposite points of pastry over the apple. Overlap, moisten, seal, and place in 9 x 13 inch pan. Pour hot syrup around dumplings. Bake immediately in 425° F. oven for 40 to 50 minutes or until crust is nicely brown. Serve warm with cream or milk.

Becky Schweizer
Schweizer Orchard
Amazonia, Missouri

APFELKUCHEN

Crust
4 tablespoons butter
1 tablespoon vinegar
1 cup flour
1 tablespoon sugar

Filling
5-6 tart cooking apples
3/4 cup sugar
1/4 teaspoon cinnamon
1 tablespoon butter

Mix crust ingredients by cutting in butter and vinegar into flour and sugar with pastry blender. Mix lightly with fork. Press mixture into 9 inch pie pan.

Mix filling ingredients, put in crust, and dot with butter. Bake 15 minutes at 400° F., then 35 minutes at 350° F.

Anderson Farm Orchard
Zion, Illinois

Arneson Orchard
Blair, Wisconsin

If the kids want a ride on a tractor-pulled wagon through the orchards, Arneson Orchard can provide it. This is a fun, but bumpy way to experience the great outdoors. However, it is a good way to see and smell the richness of the apple harvest.

During picking season the orchard is brimming with apple pickers as the orchard is 95% pick-your-own. They also sell packed apples ready to go. Fresh apple cider is another product available during the apple season.

APPLE SQUARES

6 to 10 apples, peeled and sliced
1 cup sugar
1 tablespoon cornstarch
1 cup water
Cinnamon

Pastry for 2 crust pie

Make your favorite double crust pie recipe. Roll out 1/2 of dough and fit into bottom and up sides of 9 x 13 inch pan. Fill with apples. Combine sugar and cornstarch in saucepan. Blend in water. Cook, stirring constantly until thickened. Pour over apples. Sprinkle with cinnamon. Place rolled out remaining dough over apples. Seal edges. Cut slits for steam. Bake at 400° F. for 10 minutes, then at 350° F. for 20 - 30 minutes until apples are tender and crust is golden brown. If desired, frost with icing when nearly cool.

Agatha Arneson
Arneson Orchard
Blair, Wisconsin

APPLE PASTRY

2 cups flour
1/2 teaspoon salt
1 cup Crisco™
2 beaten egg yolks
1 tablespoon lemon juice
7-8 tablespoons ice water

10 apples
1 cup sugar
1 tablespoon flour
1/2 teaspoon cinnamon
1/4 teaspoon salt

Sift dry ingredients. Cut in shortening. Combine egg yolks, lemon juice, and water. Add to shortening and flour mixture. Make into ball and refrigerate while peeling apples.

Peel apples and slice. Mix sugar, 1 tablespoon flour, cinnamon, and salt. Mix through apples. Cut pastry in half. Roll out to fit 9 x 13 inch pan. Fill with apple mixture. Top with other one-half of pastry. Bake at 400° F. for 45 minutes. While warm, frost with 1 tablespoon melted butter, 1 cup confectioners' sugar, and enough warm cream to reach drizzle consistency.

Gayle M. Dracht
In memory of her late father, William Westmaas
Marion, Michigan

DESSERTS

Fruit Haven Orchard
Aspers, Pennsylvania

Fruit Haven Orchard has been a full time business for 30 years. Myles and Dorothy Starner began their orchard in 1950 and are now passing it on to their son, Neil. Their family of 4 daughters and one son all worked hard in the orchard as they were growing up. It was also a time for apple pageants and festivities, with the girls being chosen as state and county apple queens and state cherry queens.

According to Mr. Starner, Fruit Haven Orchard is very small compared to others in Adams county. They have 30 acres of fruit bearing trees, with about five acres being replanted. Their dwarf planting was started 23 years ago and now they are taking out the oldest full dwarfs and replanting dwarfs. Mr. Starner said, "It used to be that a grower only planted one set of trees in a lifetime, but at age 68, I'm planting trees for the third time."

QUICK EASY MICROWAVE APPLE DESSERT

6 to 8 cups peeled, sliced apples
1/4 cup brown sugar
1/2 cup flour
1/3 cup brown sugar
2/3 cup quick cooking oats
1/3 cup butter or margarine
1 teaspoon cinnamon or nutmeg

Place apples and the 1/4 cup brown sugar in an 8 inch square or oblong microwave pan. Microwave about 8 minutes or until apples seem soft. Meanwhile, blend the remaining ingredients with a fork or pastry blender. Add this mixture on top of apples and microwave another 3 or 4 minutes. Makes 6 servings.

"I like to take this dessert to covered dish suppers and to 'shut-ins' or someone who has had a baby. It is one of our favorite desserts here at home and I serve it often."

Dorothy Starner
Fruit Haven Orchard
Aspers, Pennsylvania

Bingham's Orchard and Fruit Market

St. Thomas, Pennsylvania

You can browse Bingham's Gift Barn, Basket Room, and Antique Shop to find the unusual and unique gifts and keepsakes. Enjoy the nostalgia of the atmosphere where quality and pride have gone into beautifully hand crafted merchandise. Shops are open year around, seven days a week. Apples are everywhere—buy them by the bushel, basket, or truckload.

APPLE CRISP FOR MICROWAVE

6 cups sliced, peeled apples
3/4 cup brown sugar, packed
1/2 cup flour
1/3 cup brown sugar, packed
1/3 cup quick-cooking oats
1/4 cup butter
1/2 teaspoon cinnamon

Place first 2 ingredients in 8 inch square dish. Microwave (High-10) 4 minutes. With pastry blender, mix rest of ingredients. Sprinkle over top of apples. Microwave 9-12 minutes (High-10), rotating dish 1/4 turn after 5 minutes. Let stand few minutes before serving. Serves 6-8.

Betty Kriner
Bingham's Orchard
St. Thomas, Pennsylvania

Arneson Orchard
Blair, Wisconsin

Clayton and Agatha Arneson started the orchard business in 1960. Specialties of the house include *Cortland, McIntosh, Delicious, Lodi, Duchess,* and *Fenton.* The orchard takes on a different character in the fall. Apple pickers come from many miles around to sample the fruits of the season.

MICROWAVE APPLE CRISP

Approximately 6 medium apples, sliced
2/3 to 3/4 cup brown sugar, packed
1/2 cup flour
1/2 cup oatmeal
3/4 teaspoon cinnamon
3/4 teaspoon nutmeg
1/3 cup butter or margarine

Arrange apple slices in ungreased 8 inch square glass baking dish. Mix remaining ingredients and sprinkle over apples. Microwave until apples are tender —about 12 minutes. Give dish 1/4 turn half way through baking.

Agatha Arneson
Arneson Orchard
Blair, Wisconsin

Ski-Hi Fruit Farm

Baraboo, Wisconsin

As the years progressed, and to accommodate the volume of business, many improvements were made at Ski-Hi Fruit Farm. These included a new pack shed, salesroom, packing equipment, and a refrigerated cooler for apple bins. The Bassetts no longer press cider with the 1910 press, as they have a new cider room with a press equipped with a cloth and rack. This is operated by one person, with one or two additional persons bottling the cider. It is pressed daily during the rush season. Visitors are welcome to view their operations.

Gramma's fresh apple pies and apple turnovers are baked daily in **Gramma's Pie Parlour**. Caramel apples are also made and are most popular, too! There is a good selection of Wisconsin apple butter, Wisconsin cheese, Wisconsin maple syrup, jellies, jams, mustards, and popcorn.

ORANGE-COCONUT APPLE CRISP
(MICROWAVE)

6 cups sliced, pared apple
2 tablespoons orange juice
2/3 cup brown sugar
1/3 cup flour
1/2 teaspoon grated orange rind
1/3 cup butter
1 cup flaked coconut

Place sliced, pared apples in 8 x 8 inch glass baking dish. Sprinkle with orange juice. Combine brown sugar, flour, and orange rind. Cut in butter until crumbly. Add coconut and toss. Sprinkle over apples. Microwave 12 minutes. Rotate 1/2 turn after 6 minutes. Cool slightly. Spoon into dessert dishes. Top with whipped cream or a scoop of ice cream.

Betty Marie Thiessen
Ski-Hi Fruit Farm
Baraboo, Wisconsin

Mincer Orchard
Hamburg, Iowa

Jonathans continue to be the magic apple in Southwest Iowa. Each year the Mincers ship boxes of them to far away states. Fruits with their superb flavor from this area are relished by those living as far away as Florida and California.

From the beginning, Mincer orchard has had an acreage devoted to peaches — though Iowa's sometimes frigid temperatures occasionally kill the tender fruit buds. Iowa's climate enhances and makes a home-grown peach a fruit to savor. They also grow strawberries, melons, sweet corn, and pumpkins, along with many other seasonal fruits.

The Mincers apple cider is acclaimed by judges to be among the very best. They wash and select the apples to be pressed and the juice is cooled in modern stainless steel equipment. Years of experience have taught them how to blend the right proportion of sweet and tart apples to produce a pure apple juice with no preservatives or additives. Their products are not only good, but good for you!

MINCER'S APPLE CRISP

7-8 cups sliced apples
1 tablespoon Minute™ tapioca
1/2 cup sugar
Cinnamon to taste
1/4 cup bread crumbs
1/2 cup quick oats
1/2 cup brown sugar
1/2 cup flour
1/8 teaspoon baking powder
1/8 teaspoon baking soda
1/4 cup butter
Pinch of salt

Pare, core, and slice apples. Layer half of the apples in a 9 x 13 inch pan. Sprinkle with tapioca. Next, sprinkle sugar and cinnamon on apples. Add rest of the sliced apples. Sprinkle the bread crumbs over the apples. Cut butter into dry ingredients and then spread over the top of the apple mixture. Bake at 375° F. for 35 to 45 minutes. Serves 8.

Ed Mincer
Mincer Orchard
Hamburg, Iowa

185

Krueger's Orchard
Godfrey, Illinois

Jonathans, Red and *Yellow Delicious, Romes,* and *Arkansas Black* apples are grown at Krueger's Orchard. Every apple, peach, pie cherry, and pear is hand picked and hand sorted. Sweet apple cider is also produced at the orchard.

The Kruegers began selling apples in 1982 and their business has been growing every year. Mr. and Mrs. Krueger and their six children have their work cut out for them for many years to come. Jo Ann Krueger commented, "We think this is one of the best places to live, work, and raise a family."

KRUEGER'S APPLE CRISP

8 cups thin sliced apples
1/2 cup sugar
1/2 cup butter or margarine
1 cup flour
3/4 cup sugar
1/2 cup brown sugar
1/2 teaspoon cinnamon

Butter 9 x 13 inch pan. Place sliced apples in pan. Sprinkle with 1/2 cup sugar. Make topping by cutting butter or margarine into flour, sugar, brown sugar, and cinnamon. Spread topping on apples. Bake at 375° F. for 30 - 40 minutes or until apples are tender.

Jo Ann Krueger
Krueger's Orchard
Godfrey, Illinois

The Apple Barn at Hope Orchards

Hope, Maine

Travel the coast to the Apple Barn at Hope Orchards, located just six miles from the ocean. The orchard features 15 different apple varieties, as well as 5 varieties of pears and peaches.

QUICK APPLE DESSERT

1/2 cup butter
1/2 cup brown sugar, packed
1 cup flour
2 teaspoons cinnamon
3 tablespoons water
1/2 cup chopped nuts
4 large apples, peeled and sliced
(*McIntosh* or *Cortland*)
1/2 cup sugar

Cream butter and brown sugar until pale and fluffy. Stir in flour, 1 teaspoon cinnamon, and water until smooth and thick. Add nuts. Mound apples in 9 inch pie plate. Mix sugar and 1 teaspoon cinnamon and sprinkle over apples. Spoon batter over apples. Bake at 375° F. for 45-50 minutes until apples are tender. Serve warm or cold with ice cream or whipped cream. Yield: 8 servings.

Linda and Karl Drechsler
The Apple Barn at Hope Orchards
Hope, Maine

The Pike's
Apples-N-Cider
Sparta, Michigan

Antique tractors abound at Pike's Apple Orchard. Farmalls C, H, A, and others are on display. There are tractors for the kids or grown-ups to sit on as they munch apples or take pictures of the beautiful countryside. Apples hanging on the trees amidst the well mowed rows make a lovely picture, indeed.

Jon and Marilyn Pike have a "hobby" orchard, with only about four acres of trees. They raise *McIntosh, Jonathan, Ida Red, Rome, Empire, Golden Delicious, Spies, Cortland,* and *Red Delicious* apples. Crafts are also featured at their retail market and they always have hot spiced cider to sample. Following are two of their special recipes.

ALL-TIME FAVORITE APPLE CRISP

10-12 apples
(*Jonathan* or *McIntosh*)
1 1/2 cups sugar
1 tablespoon cinnamon
1 tablespoon flour

Topping
1 stick butter or margarine
1 cup flour
1 cup sugar
1 cup oatmeal

Fill 9 x 13 pan 3/4 full of peeled and sliced apples; top with sugar, cinnamon, and flour. Mix dry ingredients for topping and cut in butter or margarine. Spoon topping mixture over apples. Bake at 350° F. for about 1 hour, or until apples are tender. Serve warm with ice cream.

CROCKPOT APPLESAUCE

Apples - crockpot full
(*Jonathan, McIntosh, Ida Red, Cortland*, and *Golden Delicious* are great for this)
1/2 cup water or cider
1 teaspoon cinnamon
1/2 cup sugar
1/4 cup cinnamon candies, optional

Put all ingredients into crockpot. Cover and cook 8-10 hours on low or 3-4 hours on high heat.

"I like to add cinnamon candies for a nice pink color."

Marilyn Pike
The Pike's Apples-N-Cider
Sparta, Michigan

Fireside Orchard and Gardens
Northfield, Minnesota

Robert and Judy Harvey are the third generation of apple growers in their family. They pride themselves on growing the finest Minnesota apples. They are located near Carleton and St. Olaf Colleges in Northfield.

Fireside Orchard and Gardens have beautiful mums and other flower gardens for their customers to enjoy. Several unique Minnesota varieties, such as *Haralson, Regent, Honey Crisp,* and *Fireside* are among the ten different varieties of apples grown. They also have fresh pressed cider, home-made donuts and fudge, along with honey/maple syrup, jams and jellies, and Minnesota cheeses.

OUR FAVORITE APPLE CRISP

1 cup brown sugar
1 1/2 cups flour
3/4 teaspoon baking powder
1/2 teaspoon salt
1/2 cup melted butter or margarine
6-8 raw tart apples, sliced
1 cup sugar
1 1/2 teaspoons cinnamon

Blend brown sugar, flour, baking powder, and salt. Stir in butter or margarine until mixture is crumbly. Combine apples, sugar, and cinnamon. Spread the apple mixture in a 9 x 13 inch pan and cover with the crumbly mixture. Bake at 350° F. for 30 minutes or until golden brown.

Judy Harvey
Fireside Orchard and Gardens
Northfield, Minnesota

Bob's
Bluebird Orchard
and Gardens

LINDA'S FAVORITE APPLE CRISP

1/2 cup butter or margarine
1 cup flour
3/4 cup sugar
1 teaspoon cinnamon
6 medium apples
1/2 cup water

Blend butter or margarine, flour, sugar, and cinnamon until well mixed and crumbly. Peel apples and slice into buttered 8 x 8 inch baking dish. Add water, then cover with first mixture. Bake 30 minutes at 350° F. to 375° F.

"Topping also good as top crust on pie for Dutch Apple Pie."

Bob and Linda Leis
Bob's Bluebird Orchard
Webster, Minnesota

Emma Krumbee's Restaurant, Apple Orchard, Bakery, Deli, & Country Store

Belle Plaine, Minnesota

Emma's Apple Barn is a favorite spot to stop and pick up a bag or a bushel of crisp, juicy apples. Or you may be drawn in by the aroma of homemade baked goods, such as pies, cookies, pastries, donuts, and coffee cakes. Whatever the season, the Apple Barn offers a spectacular view of Emma Krumbees.

The Apple Orchard at Emma Krumbee's has all the old-fashioned apple types as well as the newest apple varieties such as *Redfrees,* an acid-free apple, and several crossbreeds such as *Williams Pride* and *Jonamacs.* With 7,500 apple trees yielding 24 varieties, Emma Krumbee's Apple Orchard is ideal for "u-picking".

A fall tradition at Emma Krumbee's is the Great Scarecrow Festival, which draws thousands of spectators every year. Scarecrow creators of all ages from across the state compete for cash prizes in traditional, humorous, and contemporary categories. Nearly 100 figures are on display throughout October. Scarecrow festivities include children's games, hay pile jump, human size hay maze, and "u-pick" pumpkins in Emma's 8 acre Great Pumpkin Patch.

APPLE KRUMBEE CRISP

8 cups sliced apples
(*Haralson* or *Granny Smith*)
1 teaspoon cinnamon
1 1/2 cups brown sugar
1 1/2 cups flour
1 cup butter
2 cups oatmeal
1 teaspoon salt

Mix in cinnamon with apples. Place in a greased 9 x 13 inch pan. Combine brown sugar, flour, butter, and oatmeal. Mix until crumbly-like consistency forms (similar to a streusel topping). Pour "crumbly" topping over the apples. Bake at 350° F. for 35 to 40 minutes.

"Excellent with cinnamon ice cream!"

Mark Sauter, Head Baker
Emma Krumbee's Restaurant, Bakery, Deli and Apple Orchard
Belle Plaine, Minnesota

Susan Ochs' recipes are dedicated to the memory of her late husband, Leslie, who passed away in June, 1994. He so devoted his life to their apple orchard. She and their son, Alan, now operate the farm.

OCHS' APPLE CRISP

Apples to fill 8-inch square pan
(*MacIntosh* and *Cortland* mixed)
1 cup sugar
3/4 cup flour
1/2 cup butter
Cinnamon
Whipped cream or ice cream

Preheat oven to 350° F. to 375° F. Slice apples, filling 8-inch square pan 3/4 full. Sprinkle cinnamon over apples. Mix sugar, flour, and butter with a fork until crumbly. Spread the mixture over the top of the apples. Bake in preheated oven for 45 minutes or until brown on top and tender when fork is inserted in apples. Serve slightly warm with whipped cream or ice cream.

Susan Ochs
Ochs Orchard
Warwick, New York

ADAE'S APPLE CRISP

4 to 6 cups sliced pared, tart apples
(*Melrose* variety is a good choice)
2/3 to 3/4 cup brown sugar, packed
1/2 cup flour
1/2 cup oats
3/4 teaspoon cinnamon
3/4 teaspoon nutmeg
1/3 cup butter or margarine, softened

Heat oven to 375° F. Grease square pan, 9 x 9 x 2 inches. Place apple slices in pan. Mix remaining ingredients thoroughly. Sprinkle over apples. Bake for 30 minutes in 375° F. oven, or until apples are tender and topping is golden brown. Serve warm and, if desired, with light cream or ice cream.

Alice Adae
A & M Farm
Midland, Ohio

Stark Brothers Nurseries and Orchards Company

Louisiana, Missouri

The discovery of the Delicious apple altered the course of the history of the Stark nurseries, making the word "Delicious" an international name for great tasting fruit.

Searching for a more perfect apple, an Apple Show and Contest was sponsored by Stark Nurseries in 1892. Growers brought their best fruit to the show. In the testing process, Clarence Stark bit into a red, rather elongated apple with five small bumps on the blossom end, and exclaimed, "Delicious! Who sent them?" However, the grower could not be found. The next year another contest was sponsored, in the hopes of again finding the best apple. This time the apple grower was identified.

The tree bearing the extra-ordinary red apple came from the farm of Jesse Hiatt of Winterset, Iowa. Stark purchased its sole rights, named the apple "Stark Delicious", and secured a registered trade mark. It became the world's most popular and profitable apple.

A nature-bred chance seedling that became almost as popular as the Stark Red Delicious was the Stark Golden Delicious. It was first found growing in the rugged mountains of West Virginia in 1915. A handful of scions was taken back to Missouri and soon the nurseries were producing this apple, which continues to rival the popularity of the Red Delicious.

APPLE CRANBERRY CRISP

3 cups sliced apples
8 oz. can jellied cranberry sauce
1/2 teaspoon grated orange rind
1 cup oatmeal
1/2 cup flour
1/2 cup brown sugar
1/2 teaspoon cinnamon
Pinch of salt
1/3 cup butter

Mix apples, cranberry sauce, and orange rind in greased 8 x 8 inch pan. Combine remaining ingredients in bowl of food processor and turn on and off until crumbly. Pour crumb topping over apple mixture. Bake at 350° F. for 45 minutes or until browned.

Ann Steele
Independence, Missouri

Kickapoo Orchard, Inc.
Gays Mills, Wisconsin

Kickapoo Orchard, Inc., purchased in 1964 by the Meyer family—Bill, Marlene, and son, Andy—is planted on ridges above the Kickapoo River, near Gays Mills, Wisconsin. Approximately 60 thousand bushels of apples are grown each year on 160 acres of orchard land.

Apples are packed both for wholesale and retail. Over 40 varieties are grown. The orchard produces its own apple cider. Their salesroom includes an apple gift shop and a bakery with a sit-down area.

KICKAPOO APPLE PIZZA

Pastry for single crust pie

3 medium baking apples

Topping 1
1 teaspoon cinnamon
1/4 cup sugar

Topping 2
1/4 cup flour
1/4 cup sugar
1/4 cup oatmeal
1/4 cup butter or margarine
1/8 cup nuts, chopped

Topping 3
1 commercial microwaveable
caramel dip - any brand

Roll pastry for single crust pie into a circle. Place flat on a greased and floured 10-inch pizza pan, or cookie sheet. Pare and core apples, then cut into 1/4-inch thick slices. Spread slices evenly over crust, spreading out to the edges. Add topping 1, 2, and 3.

Topping 1: Mix cinnamon and sugar together and spread on apples.

Topping 2: Place dry ingredients and butter or margarine into mixing bowl. Cut in with a pastry blender until fine. Mix in chopped nuts. Sprinkle mixture on top of apples, pressing mixture down on the apples evenly across the pizza. Place in pre-heated 375° F. oven. Bake until lightly browned and bubbling, approximately 30 minutes. Remove from oven and allow to cool on the pan about 5 minutes. Cut into 8 pieces, using pizza cutter or a knife. Microwave the caramel, following directions for that brand, then drizzle the warmed caramel over the top of the pizza. Using pie-wedge spatula, remove to dessert plates and serve.

M. Marlene Meyer
Kickapoo Orchard, Inc.
Gays Mills, Wisconsin

Soergel Orchards
Wexford, Pennsylvania

To get to Soergel Orchards take the Wexford exit of Interstate 79 north of Pittsburg. They are open all year around.

Warren and Jean Soergel and family are the current owners. The original farm was started in 1850 and the fifth generation is now working the farm. Their first retail farm market was built in 1960.

At Christmas time, apples are shipped all over the USA and hundreds of fruit baskets are made. The orchard's bakery never stops baking pies for the holidays.

— SOERGELS ORCHARDS —

SOERGEL'S APPLE PIZZA

Pastry for single crust pie

2/3 cup sugar
3 tablespoons flour
1 teaspoon cinnamon

4 medium baking apples, peeled and cut into 1/2 inch slices

Topping
1/2 cup flour
1/3 cup brown sugar, packed
1/3 cup rolled oats
1 teaspoon cinnamon
1/4 cup softened butter or margarine
1/4-1/2 cup caramel ice cream topping or
    caramel apple dip
Vanilla ice cream, optional

Roll pastry to fit 12-inch pizza pan. Fold under or flute edges. Combine sugar, flour, and cinnamon in a bowl. Add apples and toss. Arrange apples in single layer in a circular pattern to cover pastry. Combine first 5 topping ingredients. Sprinkle over apples. Bake at 350° F. for 35-40 minutes until apples are tender. Remove from oven and immediately drizzle with caramel. Serve warm with ice cream or whipped topping, if desired.

Linda Voll
Soergel Orchards
Wexford, Pennsylvania

Hugus Fruit Farm
Rushville, Ohio

Hugus Fruit Farm is in an area where Johnny Appleseed "passed through." This is a family owned and customer oriented apple operation. The orchard was established in 1944 and is now being managed by the third generation.

Eight varieties of apples are raised in the orchard. *Melrose,* an "Ohio apple," has become very popular. School groups like to tour the orchard and see the grading and storage of apples and the cider press in operation.

One of the specialities of Hugus Fruit Farm is their apple butter. It is made in copper kettles over an open fire. They have been making apple butter for over 35 years.

HUGUS' APPLE PIZZA

Crust
2 cups flour
1 tablespoon sugar
1/2 cup vegetable oil
1/4 cup cold water
1/4 teaspoon salt

4 cooking apples, peeled, cored, sliced
(*Melrose, Winesap, Granny Smith*)

Topping
1/2 cup butter or margarine (1 stick)
1/2 cup granulated sugar
1/2 cup brown sugar
3/4 cup flour
1 teaspoon cinnamon

To make crust, mix dry ingredients, stir in oil and water. Pat into 12 inch greased pizza pan. Place sliced apples on crust.

Mix topping into a crumbly mixture and sprinkle over apples. Bake at 375° F. for 20-25 minutes.

Joan Hugus
Hugus Fruit Farm
Rushville, Ohio

MINI APPLE PIZZA

1 tube refrigerated biscuits
2 yellow *Delicious* apples, peeled and grated
1/4 cup brown sugar, packed
1 tablespoon flour
1 teaspoon cinnamon
Mozzarella cheese

Place biscuits in jelly roll pan. Pat in 3 1/2 inch circles. Mix other ingredients, dividing equally over the 10 biscuits. Top with mozzarella cheese. Bake at 350° F. for about 20 minutes. Yield: 10 servings.

Laura Hershberger
Hillcrest Orchard
Walnut Creek, Ohio

AUTUMN HARVEST CHEESECAKE

Crust
1 cup graham cracker crumbs
3 tablespoons sugar
1/2 teaspoon cinnamon
3 tablespoons butter or margarine, melted

Filling
8 oz. cream cheese, softened
1/2 cup sugar
2 eggs
1/2 teaspoon vanilla
4 cups apples, peeled and thinly sliced
1/3 cup sugar
1/2 teaspoon cinnamon
1/2 cup chopped pecans

Combine crumbs, sugar, cinnamon, and butter or margarine; press onto bottom of 9 inch springform pan. Bake at 350° F. for 10 minutes.

Combine cream cheese and sugar, mixing at medium speed on electric mixer until well blended. Add eggs, 1 at a time, mixing well after each addition. Blend in vanilla; pour over crust. Toss apples with combined sugar and cinnamon. Spoon apple mixture over cream cheese layer; sprinkle with pecans.

Bake at 350° F. for 1 hour and 10 minutes. Loosen cake from rim of pan; cool before removing rim of pan. Chill. Yields 10-12 servings.

"The orchard life is alot of manual labor, but it also provides a backdrop for a very satisfying lifestyle. Unquestionably, the greatest satisfaction comes from the association with our customers."

Colleen Carlson
Carlsons Orchard and Farm Bakery
Winsted, Minnesota

Bayfield Apple Company
Bayfield, Wisconsin

Bayfield Apple Company is a family farm orchard located on a microclimate area in the northern-most section of Wisconsin. This 1 x 4 mile plateau area is 600 feet above Lake Superior overlooking the Apostle Islands in the Town of Bayfield. The islands act as huge breakwaters to calm the rolling waters of Lake Superior so the surface water can warm in the summer. Prevailing westerly winds are inverted from these waters over the plateau, resulting in a controlled climate with a longer growing season.

This microclimate was "discovered" in 1900, and by 1912 had the largest apple production in Wisconsin. Production declined after WW1 as other more populated areas began producing. Their apple production now is but a fraction of what it once was, however Bayfield can still boast of having the largest Apple Festival in the state. The festival attracts more than 30,000 people to this snug little harbor town, so small there is not even one stop light in the whole county! Their apple production may be down from former times, but their level of fun is still at an all time high.

APPLE FRITTERS

1 egg, beaten
1 cup milk
1 cup finely chopped, unpeeled, cored apple
(*Cortland* - good choice)
1/4 cup sugar
1/4 teaspoon salt
3 tablespoons orange juice
1 teaspoon grated orange peel
1/2 teaspoon vanilla
2 cups sifted flour
3 teaspoons baking powder

Sifted confectioners' sugar

Combine first eight ingredients. Sift flour and baking powder together. Fold this into the first mixture, stirring JUST until flour is moistened.

Drop by rounded TEASPOONS (make small) into deep hot fat (350° F.). When fritters rise to surface, turn and fry until a deep golden brown. Takes about 3 minutes.

Drain thoroughly on paper towels and then roll in sifted confectioners' sugar. Serve hot.

Fritters can be frozen for later use. Reheat in microwave immediately before serving.

"This recipe came from my wife's mother many years ago. It is the #1 request at our house by myself and children."

Einar Olsen
Bayfield Apple Company
Bayfield, Wisconsin

Bauman Orchard, Inc.

Rittman, Ohio

Started in 1929 by Ben Bauman, the Bauman Orchard, Inc. is a 3-family operated business now owned by Marion, Doug, and Bill Bauman. The original purchase consisted of 10 acres of orchard, with 30 more acres added in 1935. In 1942, 50 acres were planted, some of which are still in production today.

In 1961, Ben Bauman's son, Marion, purchased the business. Various plantings were made over the years. A partnership was formed in 1987 with Doug coming into the business and later joined by Bill in 1990. By 1992, 117 acres were devoted to fruit production, with approximately 8000 apple trees, 2000 peach trees, and a few plum and pear trees.

Ninety percent of the orchard business is wholesale, with a small retail farm market open all year. Apples are available the year around.

Pick-your-own apples are featured the first 3 Saturdays of October, with wagon rides, pony rides, hot dogs and cider, and various other fun activities. Starting in September, school tours are given. An array of fruit baskets are offered during the holidays. There is always something going on at the orchard!

APPLE DELIGHT

1/4 cup melted butter
1/8 teaspoon cinnamon
1 cup graham cracker crumbs
1/4 cup brown sugar
8 oz. cream cheese
1 teaspoon vanilla
1 cup confectioners' sugar
1/2 pint whipping cream
2-3 cups cooked *Ida Red* apples
Graham cracker crumbs for topping

Mix butter, cinnamon, graham cracker crumbs, and sugar. Press into bottom of 9 x 9 inch pan. Bake at 325° F. for 10 minutes. Cool. Cream 8 oz. of cream cheese; add vanilla and confectioners' sugar, beating until fluffy. Whip cream in separate bowl and blend into cream cheese mixture. Spread over crumb crust. Arrange cooked apple slices over cream cheese mixture. Sprinkle graham cracker crumbs over apple slices. Chill overnight.

Dianna Bauman
Bauman Orchards, Inc.
Rittman, Ohio

Dunn's Cider Mill
Belton, Missouri

The tradition of cider sipping goes back to the early years of this century in the Dunn family. Every autumn Grandfather Willis Chapin Dunn, along with his five children, would hitch up a wagon and head up the hill to the orchard that overlooked the farm in upstate New York. Everyone picked apples until the wagon was overflowing. Then they would stop at a grist mill with a press that squeezed cider from the apples. A wagon load would fill two or three barrels.

When the family returned to the farm, one barrel was left outdoors for the children to sip. They would then frantically search in the barn loft for suitable stalks of straw with hollow centers. There was much juggling for position when the bung— somewhat like a wooden cork—was removed from the barrel. By late afternoon the level inside the barrel had been lowered to the point where it became difficult to find a straw long enough to draw more cider. Then, someone, generally the oldest, having anticipated this situation, would remove from a hiding place in the barn an exceptionally long straw found a few days earlier. He would then sip undisturbed while the others were back in the loft searching for ever longer straws.

Today the tradition of cider sipping continues, however a few changes have been made. The straws are made of plastic and everyone sips from a clean cup.

BAVARIAN APPLE TORTE

Crust
1/2 cup butter or margarine
1/3 cup sugar
1/4 teaspoon vanilla
1 cup flour

Filling
8 oz. cream cheese, softened
1/4 cup sugar
1 egg
1/2 teaspoon vanilla
1/3 cup additional sugar
1/2 teaspoon cinnamon
4 cups peeled, thinly sliced apples
1/4 cup sliced almonds

To make crust, cream butter, 1/3 cup sugar, and 1/4 teaspoon vanilla. Blend in flour. Spread dough onto bottom and about 1 1/2 inches up sides of 9-inch springform pan.

To make filling, combine cream cheese and 1/4 cup sugar; mix well. Stir in egg and 1/2 teaspoon vanilla. Pour into pastry-lined pan.

Combine 1/3 cup sugar and cinnamon. Toss apple slices in sugar mixture. Spoon apple mixture over cream cheese layer; sprinkle with sliced almonds.

Bake 10 minutes at 450° F. Reduce heat to 400° F. and continue baking 25 minutes. (If torte appears to be browning too quickly, cover loosely with aluminum foil during last 10 to 15 minutes of baking time.) Cool without removing rim of pan. Makes 8 to 10 servings.

Dunn's Cider Mill
Belton, Missouri

Cold Hollow Cider Mill

Waterbury Center, Vermont

A small bakery added to the Cold Hollow Cider Mill makes baklava, fruit cakes, maple granola and other products, using only fresh Vermont butter, organic whole grains, and Vermont eggs. Their products do not contain additives or preservatives.

When the autumn days are crisp and cool, the Chittendens press crisp, tart apples into fresh cider. This then gets boiled down and made into their Pure Cider Jelly, with no pectin or sugar added.

As the cider business grew, so did the Chittenden family. Francine and Eric's three children, Eliza, Lemira, and Nathaniel, are learning the finer points of running a business on a daily basis. Eliza spends several hours a week behind the retail counter, making donuts, or serving customers. Lemira helps out by baby-sitting for staff or pricing and stocking shelves. Nathaniel's biggest contribution is sampling baked goods and offering consumer advice — the perfect job for a boy his age.

APPLE TARTS

1 cup butter
1/2 cup honey
2 cups whole wheat pastry flour
1/2 tablespoon vanilla
1 1/2 pounds cream cheese
1/2 cup honey
3 eggs
1 teaspoon vanilla
3 1/2 to 4 cups apples, chopped
1/2 cup honey
1 teaspoon cinnamon

Cream butter and 1/2 cup honey. Add flour and vanilla. Pat into bottom of two 10 inch springform pans. Refrigerate. Mix cream cheese, 1/2 cup honey, eggs, and vanilla in a food processor or by hand. Spread mixture over shells in pans. Toss apples with honey and cinnamon. Arrange on top of cream cheese mixture. Bake at 350° F. for 50 minutes or until brown. Paint with cider jelly and water glaze and garnish with raisins, if desired.

Gail McCain
Cold Hollow Cider Mill
Waterbury Center, Vermont

Hauser's Superior View Farm
Bayfield, Wisconsin

Hauser's Superior View Farm is located in a picturesque area of
northern Wisconsin overlooking Lake Superior and the Apostle
Islands. Its origin is a study in a family's resourcefulness and the
ability of its founders to see opportunities when confronted with
obstacles.

In 1908 a Swiss American family named Hauser settled in
Bayfield, Wisconsin. Great-Grandfather Hauser was a gifted
horticulturist and grew strawberries and prize winning potatoes. When
the embargo on seeds from Europe began in 1928, Great Grandfather
saw this as an ideal opportunity to grow and sell perennial flowers and
straw-flowers. This soon became a very profitable business and even
today, Hauser's Superior View Farm is one of the largest producers of
northern field grown perennials in the country. Every spring and fall
shipments are made all over the United States.

In 1928, in the depth of the great depression, Grandfather Hauser
started his first apple orchard as a way to make extra income. A few
years later, he added the famous original *Knight* orchard with those
wonderful *Dudley* apples. Since then, many changes have occurred.
Now, Hausers have about 2,000 apple trees on 30 acres and grow
varieties such as *McIntosh,* and *Cortland,* and those still wonderful
Dudley apples. James, Sr. and Marilyn Hauser are the current owners,
along with their son, Jim, who is following in his father's,
grandfather's, and great-grandfather's footsteps.

In 1988, Hauser's began a jam kitchen called **A Little Bit of
Country**. From there you can find such delectable delights as
blackberry, blueberry, strawberry, peach, and cherry jam. You can
also find plum jelly, raspberry jelly, and apple butter. A big hit has
been apple syrup, which also makes a mouth-watering ice cream
topping. Everything in **A Little Bit of Country** is homemade, locally
grown, and state approved.

214

CHEESE BARS

2 packages Pillsbury™ crescent rolls
(8 in package)
2 - 8 oz. packages cream cheese
1 cup sugar
1 egg, separated
1 teaspoon vanilla

Topping
1/2 cup sugar
1 teaspoon cinnamon
1/2 cup chopped nuts
1/2 cup chopped apples

Mix cream cheese, sugar, egg yolk, and vanilla until smooth.
Stretch 1 package crescent rolls in bottom of ungreased 9 x 13 inch
pan. Spread cream cheese mixture on rolls. Stretch second package
crescent rolls on counter to pan dimensions. Lay on top of cream
cheese mixture. Beat egg whites until frothy. Brush on top of rolls,
using all of the egg white. Sprinkle with topping. Bake at 350° F. for
30 minutes.

Marilyn Hauser
Hauser's Superior View Farm
Bayfield, Wisconsin

OZARK PUDDING

2 eggs
1 cup sugar
4 tablespoons flour
2 1/2 teaspoons baking powder
2 teaspoons vanilla
2 cups chopped tart apples
1 cup chopped nuts

Preheat oven to 350° F. Beat eggs; sift dry ingredients and add to eggs. Stir in vanilla, apples, and nuts. Pour into greased 9 x 13 inch pan. Bake at 350° F. for 30 to 35 minutes. Serve warm or cold.

"Delicious!"

Sarah Brown
The Apple Works
Trafalgar, Indiana

Hollabaugh Bros., Inc. Fruit Farms and Market

Biglerville, Pennsylvania

Hollabaugh farm was originally bought in 1955 by the two elder Hollabaugh Bros., who happen to be twins. In 1982, the three sons of one of the twins joined the partnership, at which time the corporation — Hollabaugh Bros., Inc.— was born. Currently third generation children are becoming of the age to take an active part. Whether they will continue the tradition into the next century is yet to be seen.

APPLE SURPRISE

3 cups unsweetened applesauce
1 cup raisins
2 cups bread crumbs
1 cup brown sugar
1/2 cup butter
1 cup chopped nuts
18 marshmallows

Put applesauce in 9 x 13 inch baking pan. Add raisins and dot with whole marshmallows. In saucepan, melt butter. Add bread crumbs to butter to evenly coat. Add brown sugar and nuts. Heat until sugar coats the crumbs. Sprinkle this mixture over applesauce-raisins-marshmallow mixture. Bake at 375° F. for 20 to 25 minutes.

Kay E. Hollabaugh
Hollabaugh Bros., Inc.
Fruit Farms & Market
Biglerville, Pennsylvania

DeLong Orchard
Eagleville, Missouri

The first commercial orchard was planted on this property in 1898. The 40 acre orchard was purchased in 1910 by John F. DeLong. Three orchards and three generations later the DeLong family is still growing apples. Darwin and Virginia DeLong are the present owners.

The orchard currently consists of 15 acres of dwarf and semi-dwarf trees. Their main crops include *Jonathan, Grimes Golden*, and *Red* and *Yellow Delicious*. Fresh cider is made from their apples.

The DeLongs have always produced for a local market. With a declining rural population and a change in buying habits, the local market has declined and so has the acreage. The DeLongs have seen many changes in the past forty nine years that they have operated the family orchards.

CIDER PUDDING

2 cups cider
4 tablespoons cornstarch
2 tablespoons sugar
2 tablespoons red hot cinnamon candy

Measure ingredients and bring to boil in quart size saucepan, stirring all the while to keep smooth and free from lumps. Makes 4 servings.

Virginia DeLong
DeLong Orchard
Eagleville, Missouri

APPLE PUDDING

5 or 6 medium size apples
(tart and firm apples such as *Jonathans* are good choice)
3/4 cup raisins

Cider pudding
3 tablespoons flour
1 tablespoon sugar
1 cup cider

Cake dough
1 cup flour
1/2 stick butter or margarine
1/2 cup brown sugar
1/4 cup milk

In water, soak the washed raisins while preparing the cider pudding and cake dough.

To make cider pudding, mix together 3 tablespoons flour, 1 tablespoon sugar, and 1 cup cider in saucepan. Stir and cook over medium heat until thick.

Wash, peel, and slice 5 or 6 medium size apples, or enough to fill a 1 1/2 quart size casserole dish 3/4 full. Sprinkle raisins over apples and pour cooked cider pudding over apple/raisins. Sprinkle top with a mixture of:
1/2 cup sugar
1 tablespoon cinnamon
1 1/2 teaspoons nutmeg

Mix well to coat slices of apples with the sugar/spices and cider pudding.

For cake dough, cut butter into flour and brown sugar; add milk and mix together. Spoon batter over apples and cider pudding. Bake at 350° F. for 1 hour. Cool. Serve with whipped topping and top with red hot cinnamon candy. Makes five servings.

Virginia DeLong
DeLong Orchard
Eagleville, Missouri

Betzold's Orchards
Bayfield, Wisconsin

In 1922, Ed Betzold and partner, Joe Thom, started the farm that is now home to Betzold's Orchard. The orchard was planted in 1924. After buying out his partner, Ed continued farming and keeping the orchard going.

Ed Betzold married Josephine Dauk in 1924 and a year later they had their first child, Eugene. As an expansion to their farming operation, a dairy was started in 1936, with milk being delivered to the local town. The dairy was stopped in 1950.

More fruit was planted, especially strawberries and cherries and the orchard of 1100 trees was maintained. In 1955, Betzold's son, Eugene, became a partner in the orchard business. That year he married Viola Schrauth.

In 1957, a new orchard of 8 acres was planted and another in 1959. A plant for peeling and coring apples was installed and new freezers were added. In 1982, another orchard was planted, making a total of 35 acres.A number of varieties of apples are grown, such as *Wealthy, Northwest Greening, Cortland, McIntosh,* and *Connell Red.* Apples can be purchased frozen in 30 pound tins, as well as other more conventional ways.

APPLE TORTE

Crust
2 cups flour
1 cup shortening or
1/2 cup butter and 1/2 cup Crisco™
2 tablespoons sugar
pinch of salt

12 apples
1 cup sugar
1 teaspoon cinnamon

Custard
3 egg yolks, well beaten
2 cups milk
1/4 cup sugar
2 tablespoons cornstarch

Meringue
3 egg whites, beaten stiff
1/2 cup sugar

For crust, mix together like for pie crust, but do not add any water. Line bottom and sides of 9 x 12 inch pan with mixture. Pat and smooth into pan with hands. Peel and then slice 12 apples over crust mixture; sprinkle sugar and cinnamon on apples. Bake until apples are done, about 1 hour, at 350° F. Let cool.

Make custard by mixing together the well beaten egg yolks, milk, and sugar-cornstarch mixture. Cook in saucepan over medium heat until thick. When cool, pour over apples. Make meringue by beating 3 egg whites until stiff; slowly adding in 1/2 cup sugar. Spread over custard and brown in oven. Cut in squares.

Viola Betzold
Betzold's Orchards
Bayfield, Wisconsin

APPLE CRISP IN A HURRY

6 apples, peeled and sliced
1 cup sugar
1 cup Bisquick™
1/2 cup (1 stick) butter or margarine

Slice apples into bottom of 9 x 9 inch pan. Sprinkle with cinnamon and 2 tablespoons of water. In another bowl, mix 1 cup of sugar and 1 cup Bisquick™. Melt butter or margarine and add to Bisquick™ and sugar. Mix as for pie crust crumbles. Add mixture to top of apples and bake about 40 minutes until brown at 350° F.

Viola Betzold
Betzold's Orchard
Bayfield, Wisconsin

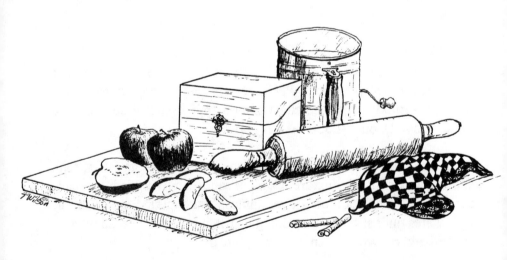

Countryside Apple Center
Kenosha, Wisconsin

With its proximity to Lake Michigan, Countryside Apple Center is located in an area that has good growing conditions. Some old varieties are grown, such as *Baldwin, Wolf River, Jonathan*, and *Delicious*. New varieties include *Gala* and *JonaGold*. The disease resistant varieties of *JonaFree, Prima*, and *Pricilla* also grown in their orchard produce fruit worthy of any fine connoisseur taste discrimination.

SIMPLE BAKED APPLES

Apples
(*Ida Reds* are ideal)
2 tablespoons sugar per apple
1 teaspoon cinnamon per apple

Simply core apples and fill cavity with cinnamon and sugar mixture. Place in suitable dish. Microwave at 4 minutes per apple.

Carl Bullmore
Countryside Apple Center
Kenosha, Wisconsin

Orchard Hill Farm
Lowell, Michigan

Orchard Hill Farm, owned by Pamella Klahn Mack and C. B. Klahn, is located 15 miles south east of Grand Rapids, Michigan. It is a working farm with crops and livestock. Founded in 1905, the 325 acre farm is worked and managed by women.

Making scarecrows and decorating pumpkins are an exciting part of the fall season. A maze, spook house, and farm animals help to entertain children of all ages. Hay rides are also offered at the orchard. Many children's birthday parties and club meetings are hosted at the orchard.

APPLE SORBET

6 red apples
1 tablespoon lemon juice
4 cups water
3/4 cup sugar
1 teaspoon vanilla

Wash apples; cut into quarters. Leave skins on and seeds in. In saucepan, add apples, lemon juice, water, and sugar and place over high heat. Bring to a boil. Reduce heat, cover and simmer for 45 minutes. Stir in vanilla. Put through a food mill. Discard skins and seeds. Refrigerate until chilled. Pour into ice cream freezer and freeze according to directions. Yield: 1 quart sorbet

Pamella Klahn Mack
Orchard Hill Farm
Lowell, Michigan

The Apple Sellers
Darwin, Minnesota

Apple Sellers Orchard was started in the thirties by a man who cleared the twenty acre area of big trees by hand, using a cross-cut saw. The soil has grown only apples. As it is protected by a forest on two sides, the growing conditions for apples in this location are also good. A lake borders the orchard on another side, which helps warm the temperature.

Keith and Anne Sellers are the fourth owners of the orchard and each one has added to the orchard services. Some of these include making pies for sale, pressing cider, and renovating an old barn for apple sales and craft items.

There are about 30 varieties of apples grown at the orchard, located 50 miles west of Minneapolis on highway 12. Some apples ripen in August and others in September and October.

APPLE CRANBERRY DESSERT

4 1/2 cups peeled, sliced apples
3/4 cup whole cranberry sauce
1 cup brown sugar
 3/4 cup sifted flour
1 teaspoon cinnamon
6 teaspoons softened butter

Arrange peeled, sliced apples in rows in buttered 8 inch square baking dish. Spread whole cranberry sauce over top of apples. Combine in bowl: brown sugar, sifted flour, and cinnamon. Mix well. Cut in softened butter and mix until crumbly. Sprinkle this over the top. Bake at 350° F. for 35-40 minutes or until apples are tender. Cut into squares. Serve warm or cold. Top with whipped cream.

Anne Sellers
The Apple Sellers
Darwin, Minnesota

Stark Brothers Nurseries and Orchards Company
Louisiana, Missouri

The constant experimentation and testing in the research and experimental grounds keeps Stark Brothers Nurseries on the cutting edge of the latest technology in fruit propagation. Developments such as the semi-dwarf and double-dwarf trees rather than the old standard tall apple trees have revolutionized orcharding. Award winning roses and different flowers, shrubs, trees and bushes have been developed through their constant search for superior strains. The story of the Stark Brothers Nurseries and Orchards Company is one of dedication to the growth and advancement of international horticulture.

The Stark family business has been credited with being one of the oldest, if not **the** oldest company in America continuously operated by one family. And from the beginning, apples played a leading role in their success.

APPLE BREAD PUDDING

8 slices bread, toasted
1/4 cup butter or margarine
1 can apple pie filling
1/2 cup raisins
1 teaspoon cinnamon
1/4 cup brown sugar
1 cup hot water
1 cup milk
2 eggs, slightly beaten
1/2 teaspoon vanilla
1/2 teaspoon salt
Nutmeg, cheddar cheese, or whipped cream, optional

Spread toasted bread with butter or margarine; arrange 4 slices bread, buttered side up, in a well greased 9 x 9 inch pan. Spread pie filling over bread; top with raisins and cinnamon. Cut remaining bread into cubes; arrange over apples, covering entire surface. Stir brown sugar and hot water together until sugar is somewhat dissolved; then add milk, eggs, vanilla, and salt. Pour over bread. Sprinkle top with nutmeg. Bake at 350° F. for 50 to 60 minutes or until custard is set. To microwave, use High setting 15-20 minutes.

Remove from oven and sprinkle with nutmeg and/or cheese, or use the whipped topping instead. Let pudding stand 15-20 minutes before serving.

June Jennings
Stark Brothers Nursery
Middletown, Missouri

The Ridge Orchards
Bourbon, Missouri

Charles and Leona Heitsch are happy to walk through the orchard with any guests, at any time of the year, sharing what they have learned about Missouri apple culture. This differs considerably from what they have experienced growing apples in Michigan. They believe, however, that the flavor of the fruit is superb, and state, not without a bit of pride, that "the flavor of our apples is equal to the Michigan apples of our childhood, and perhaps even better!"

APPLE-BERRY SHORTCAKE

2 cups of any berries, fresh and crushed or frozen
(raspberries, strawberries, blueberries)
1 quart cooked apples (4 cups fresh apples and 1 cup water)
1/2 cup honey or maple syrup

1 1/2 cups flour
3 teaspoons baking powder
3 teaspoons butter or margarine
1 egg
1/2 cup milk

Blend butter or margarine with flour; stir in egg and milk with fewest possible strokes. Pat mixture into greased 9 inch pie pan. Bake 30 minutes at 350° F.

Crush fresh berries and add to cooked, still warm, apples. Cut shortcake into wedges, butter if you wish, place in bowl, and pour on the warm apple-berry topping. Servings: 4-6.

Leona Heitsch
The Ridge Orchards
Bourbon, Missouri

JAMS,
PRESERVES,
ETC.

Bayfield Apple Company
Bayfield, Wisconsin

Twelve varieties of apples are grown in the Bayfield Apple Company orchard. Many of the trees are more than 60 years old. Some of these old varieties are not readily available elsewhere.

Besides fresh apples and apple cider, the Bayfield Apple Company has two extra special products that attract people from near and far —these are their Apple Jam and Apple Raspberry Cider. Their fresh Apple Raspberry Cider is an exclusive cider drink. They have the largest raspberry crop in Wisconsin, providing them with a sufficient quantity of berries. The raspberries are mixed with apples chopped in their cider press and absolutely nothing else is added to make this natural drink. Apples provide all the pectin for their jams and jellies. Sugar use is reduced by using the natural fructose sugar from apples. All of their jams and jellies use these two apple ingredients rather than the commercial equivalents.

232

BAYFIELD APPLE JAM

3 1/2 pounds apples
(use firm apples and mix tart and sweet varieties)
Juice of 1 lemon (optional)
1 1/2 cups sugar
1/4 cup brown sugar
Pinch of cinnamon to taste

Peel, core, and quarter apples. Place peelings and cores in large 4 quart pan. Cover with water. Bring to a boil and then simmer for 30 minutes. Drain this liquid over apples; add the lemon juice, and cook apples until soft enough to press through a sieve to make a purée. Measure out one quart of the purée and refrigerate until ready to make the jam.

Place the drained cores and peelings into a sturdy plastic bag along with the remainder of the apples (drained) that were not needed for the quart of purée. Freeze the contents of the bag. About one hour before you are ready to make the jam, remove bag from freezer. As mix in bag thaws, slowly press melting liquid from bag until 1 1/2 cups of liquid are accumulated. Discard the balance of the contents of bag.

To make jam: Place purée in pan and cook rapidly to boiling point. Stir in sugar, the 1 1/2 cups of liquid from the freezer bag and the cinnamon. Cook rapidly to 222° F., stirring often. When completely heated to 222° F. , quickly place into sterilized jars and tighten lids. Process for 5 minutes in boiling water bath. Invert jars for 20 minutes. Makes: five 8-ounce jars.

"Use this natural jam product as a spread on toast, a meat glaze, or an ice cream topping (heated). Another interesting version: use as a filling for acorn squash. Just add to squash for the final fifteen minutes of baking."

Einar Olsen
Bayfield Apple Company
Bayfield, Wisconsin

Hugus Fruit Farm

Rushville, Ohio

APPLE BUTTER

Makes 40-50 quarts, depending on the apples, weather, and sign of the moon!

7 bushels apples, peeled, cored, and quartered
(to equal about 3 1/2 bushels prepared)
25 gallons cider
1 stick (1/4 pound) butter
4 pounds brown sugar
15-20 pounds white sugar, to taste
(varies with sweetness of apples)
Small container (1 1/4 - 1 1/2 ounces) ground cinnamon

Canning jars and lids

25 gallon copper kettle and a stirrer

Start with a 25 gallon copper kettle filled with cider. Boil this down to half the volume (over a wood fire). Add the prepared apples in small quantities until all apples are cooked up and mixture is smooth - stirring constantly. (This takes several hours.)

When the first apples are added, there is a time when they burst and foam furiously. This is when the stick of butter is added to calm the action.

Continue cooking, stirring with a figure 8 motion until apple butter is a good consistency. Add sugar gradually and carefully, stirring continually to prevent scorching.

Test for "doneness" with a large spoonful apple butter on a clean plate. Cool slightly; see if it "mounds" and that there is very little or no "weeping" of liquid from the apple butter onto the plate. (Another good test is to spread on slice of homemade bread!)

Remove from fire; add cinnamon, stirring in thoroughly. Put into prepared jars, seal. Process for 5 minutes in boiling water bath. Enjoy!

Notes from Hugus Fruit Farm: *"We often use Winesap apples - any good flavored apple is okay. Grimes Golden thicken well. We also make this with Golden Delicious apples and no added sugar and find it a very popular item in our market. We peel the apples the day before and keep them in plastic bags. It doesn't matter if they darken a little."*

Joan Hugus
Hugus Fruit Farm
Rushville, Ohio

Stephenson's Apple Tree Inn
Kansas City, Missouri

Famous for its fabulous apple fritters, old fashioned dinner rolls served with apple butter made from Stephenson orchard apples, and muffins passed in their tins, right from the oven, Stephenson's Apple Tree Inn is one of Kansas City's best known and favorite restaurants. Located just 8 miles south of Kansas City International Airport, it is near apple country and features great tasting Midwestern fare, such as hickory smoked meats that are unbelievably moist and tender. And, of course, any number of delicious apple treats are always available.

APPLE BUTTER

6 pounds apples
1 quart apple cider
1 1/4 cups sugar
2 teaspoons cinnamon
1/4 teaspoon salt
1/4 teaspoon cloves
1/4 teaspoon nutmeg

Peel 6 pounds of apples, quarter or slice. Cook with 1 quart apple cider until apples are soft, stirring often. Press through sieve or food mill. Put pulp into a large kettle. Stir in 1 1/4 cups sugar, 2 teaspoons cinnamon, 1/4 teaspoon salt, cloves, and nutmeg. Boil rapidly, stirring constantly, to prevent spattering. Continue cooking until thick enough to spread. (Pour a tablespoon hot apple butter onto chilled plate. If no rim of liquid forms around edge of apple butter, it is ready.) Pour into sterilized jars. Seal. Process for 5 minutes in boiling water bath.
Makes: 3 pints.

Steve Stephenson
Stephenson Apple Tree Inn
Kansas City, Missouri

DRYING APPLES

Tree-ripened apples are the best. Apples need to be firm and ripe for apple slice rings. Tart apples are preferred for drying and *Jonathan* is a personal favorite, with *Prairie Spy* close behind. Apples should not be picked too green and then stored, as they will not have as full a flavor.

I do not use any type of dip on my usual dried apples, and depending on the variety, they turn only a light brown. *Cortland* apples dry with very little discoloration. Even if using a variety that does turn brown, the taste is really delicious anyway. If you really prefer a white dried apple product, pretreat slices with a commercial citric acid preparation following directions, or try a lemon juice dip.

Core apples and cut them into rings, getting them as even in thickness as possible. Rings tend to dry more evenly than slices because of the more uniform size. There is no need to peel the apples first. They look and taste better with the peel on. Place rings on trays in food dehydrator following directions of the particular machine. We use electric food dehydrators and dry them to desired texture.

I prefer drying apples to the crisp stage, but before the brittle chip point. You can dry them leathery, but they will have a shorter storage life.

Dried apples should be stored in a cool, dry place. I have been successful in placing them in closed brown paper bags. For longer term storage, the best is a glass container. Do not store in the basement, unless it is very dry, and don't store on a cement floor as the dried apples pick up moisture easily.

Linda Leis
Bob's Bluebird Orchard
Webster, Minnesota

APPLE LEATHER

Place freezer bags on dryer trays. Spread applesauce thinly on the bags. Place trays in commercial food dehydrator, or outside, under screen, in full sun. When dry, strip "leather" from the freezer bags, cut into strips and store in dry place until you go on a car trip or camping expedition!

Leona Heitsch
The Ridge Orchards
Bourbon, Missouri

SPECIAL TREATS

Maplewood Orchard
Morrow, Ohio

Maplewood Orchard Country Store is open every day in the fall. Along with caramel apples, cheeses, and cider, their store is filled to the brim with honey, jams & jellies, sorghum, pop corn, maple syrup, apple butter, gourds, Indian corn, homemade bread, and lots of other goodies.

Peaches come on the market in August. Starting in mid-August, red raspberries are available. Late August heralds the ripening of white, pink and blue grapes — which are great for eating, jelly-making or wine-making. Maplewood Orchard offers the pick of the crop, whatever the season.

APPLE SPREAD

8 oz. cream cheese
1/3 cup milk
1/2 cup heavy cream
1 cup chopped tart apples
1 1/2 cups finely chopped pecans
3/4 cup finely chopped dates

Blend softened cream cheese with milk and cream. Stir in remaining ingredients. Serve with crackers or on nut breads.

Dixie A. Baker
Maplewood Orchards
Morrow, Ohio

Schweizer Orchard
Amazonia, Missouri

As one might expect, Schweizer Orchard is a busy place, especially in the fall. But the folks are not too busy to stop and talk to their friends, both old and new, who come to the orchard. Many of the same customers have been coming for many years.

Each season brings its own harmony and rhythm. Who can resist the sweet smell of apples ripening and the anticipation of that first crisp bite? The Schweizers invite you to come and experience the spirit of the season.

FRUIT DIP

8 oz. cream cheese
1 jar marshmallow creme
1/2 teaspoon vanilla

Soften cream cheese. Mix all ingredients together. Dip apple slices in lemon or orange juice to keep from turning brown. Arrange apple slices and other fruit around the dip.

Becky Schweizer
Schweizer Orchard
Amazonia, Missouri

APPLE DIP

8 oz. cream cheese
3/4 cup brown sugar
1/4 cup confectioners' sugar
1 teaspoon vanilla
2 teaspoons milk

Beat cream cheese until creamy. Beat in sugars; add vanilla and milk. Beat until mixed thoroughly. Serve with sliced apples.

This recipe comes from the apple houses and kitchens of:

Jo Ann Krueger
Krueger's Orchard
Godfrey, Illinois

Anne Sellers
The Apple Sellers
Darwin, Minnesota

Elanor and Donovan Glennie
Glennie Orchard
New Berlin, Wisconsin

ORCHARD DIRECTORY

Lyman Orchards
P.O. Box 453
Rt. 147
Middlefield, CT 06455
(203) 349-1793
Pages 142,143,144

Sanford's Sunset Orchard
P.O. Box 117, Hwy 282 W.
Ellijay, GA 30540
Pages 46,47,82,83

Krueger's Orchard
2914 Airport Rd.
Godfrey, IL 62035
Pages 172,186,242

Honey Hill Orchard
11747 Waterman Rd.
Waterman, IL 60556
(815) 264-3337
Pages 14,94,95

Anderson Farm Orchard
43245 North Green Bay Road
Zion, IL 60099
(708) 872-2918
Pages 65,174

The Apple Works
RR #3, Box 112
Trafalgar, IN 46181
(317) 878-4566
Pages 32,33,88,89,216

Mincer Orchard
1200 Willow St.
Hamburg, IA 51640
Pages 50,51,184,185

Louisburg Cider Mill, Inc.
P.O. Box 670
Louisburg, KS 66053
(913) 837-5202
Pages 78,79,80,146,147

The Apple Barn at
Hope Orchards
HC 62, Box 113, Rt. 105
Hope, ME 04847
Pages 30,31,64,187

Coon Creek Orchards
78777 Coon Creek Rd.
Armada, MI 48005
(810) 784-5062
Pages 18,19,148,149

The Apple Core Orchard
11200 E. Newburg
Durand, MI 48429
(517) 288-6065
Pages 72,73,104,105

Diehl's Orchard & Cider Mill
1479 Ranch Rd.
Holly, MI 48442
(810) 634-8981
Pages 98,99,150,151

Orchard Hill Farm Market
9896 Cascade Rd. SE
Lowell, MI 49331
(616) 868-7229
Pages 224,225

Gayle M. Dracht
20590 N. 80th Ave.
Marion, MI 49665
Page 176

The Pikes
Apples "N Cider
2627 14 Mile N.W.
Sparta, MI 49345
(616) 887-0581
Pages 188,189

Emma Krumbees Apple
    Orchard, Restaurant,
    Bakery, Deli &
    Country Store
501 E. South St.
Belle Plaine, MN 56011
(612) 873-4334
Pages 106,107,192,193

The Apple Sellers
18986 CSAH 14
Darwin, MN 55324
Pages 226,227,242

Rum River Orchard
210 St. & Hwy 169
Milaca, MN 56353
(612) 823-3354
Pages 8,9,10,28

Fireside Orchard
2225 Lonsdale Blvd.
Northfield, MN 55057
(507) 663-1376
Page 190

Bob's Bluebird Orchard &
    Craft Barn
26205 Fairlawn Ave.
Webster, MN 55088
(612) 461-3143
Pages 4,5,145,191,237

Carlsons Orchard
11893 Montgomery Ave. S.W.
Winsted, MN 55395
Pages 11,12,13,205

Schweizer Orchard
Amazonia, MO 64421
(816) 324-4641
Pages 44,70,173,241

Dunns Cider Mill
17003 Holmes Road
Belton, MO 64012
(816) 331-7214
Pages 2,3,210,211

The Ridge Orchards
HCO1 Box 66
Bourbon, MO 65441
Pages 6,26,27,45,62,63,
68,86,102,230,238

DeLong Orchard
Rt. 1
Eagleville, MO 64442
Pages 218,219

The Apple Orchard
30017 S. Lone Tree Road
Harrisonville, MO 64701
(816) 380-5177
Pages 108,109

Stephensons Apple Tree Inn
5755 N.W. Northwood Rd.
Kansas City, MO 64151
(816) 587-9300
Pages 22,23,236

Stark Bros. Nurseries &
Orchard Co.
P.O. Box 10
Louisiana, MO 63353-0010
314-754-5511
Fax 314-754-5290
Pages 66,67,112,113,114,
115,196,197,228,229

Herndon Orchard
Rt. 1, B-164 258-2501
Marionville, MO 65705
Pages 76,77

Schreiman Orchard
Rural Box 26A
Waverly, MO 64096
(816) 493-2477
Pages 52,53,60,110,111

Vaugh Orchard and
Country Store
Hwy 273
P.O. Box 145
Weston, MO 64098
(816) 386-2900
Pages 54,55,71

Morton Orchard at Arbor
Day Farm
P.O. Box 701
Nebraska City, NE 68410
(402) 873-8710 Orchard
(402) 873-9347 Tours
Pages 152,153

Alasa Farm, Inc.
P.O. Box 185
6450 Shaker Road
Alton, NY 14413-0185
(315) 483-6321
Pages 90,91

Ochs Orchard
106 Reservoir Rd.
Warwick, NY 10990
(914) 986-1591
Pages 56,57,194

Rockwell Orchards
61705 Sandy Ridge Rd.
Barnesville, OH 43713
(614) 425-2013
Pages 126,127

Hollmeyer Orchards
3241 Fiddlers Green Rd.
Cincinnati, OH 45248
Pages 120,121

Iron's Fruit Farm
1640 Stubbs Mill Rd.
Lebanon, OH 45036
(513) 932-2853
Pages 48,49,84,85,121,
154,155

Layner Orchards
Rt. 1, Box 101
Little Hocking, OH 45742
Pages 29,125

A & M Farm
22141 St. Rt. 251
Midland,OH 45148
(513) 875-2500
Pages 116,117,195

Maplewood Orchard
3728 Stubbs Mill Rd.
Morrow, OH 45152
(513) 932-7981
Pages 124,240

Bauman Orchard
161 Rittman Road
Rittman, OH 44270
(216) 925-6861
Pages 208,209

Hugus Fruit Farm
1900 Old Rushville Road
Rushville, OH 43150
Pages 202,203,234,235

The Homestead Orchard
7537 W. South Range Rd.
Salem, OH 44460-9228
Pages 81,122,123

Buckingham Orchards
8803 Cheshire Road
Sunbury, OH 43074
Pages 34,35,58,59,74,75,
100, 101

Hillcrest Orchard
2474 Township Road 444
Walnut Creek, OH 44687
Pages 118,119,204

Fruit Haven Orchard
1485 Coon Rd.
Aspers, PA 17304
(717) 677-8555
Pages 178,179

Kime's Cider Mill
171 Church St.
Bendersville, PA 17306
(717) 677-7539
Page 131

Hollabaugh Bros., Inc.
481 Carlisle Road
Biglerville, PA 17307
(717) 677-9494
Pages 42,43,217

Shatzer Fruit Market &
Orchards
21997 Lincoln Way West
Chambersburg, PA 17201
Pages 96,97,132,133

Masonic Homes Orchard
One Masonic Drive
Elizabethtown, PA 17022
(717) 361-4520
Pages 38,39,156,157

El Vista Orchards, Inc.
1160 Cold Spring Rd.
Fairfield, PA 17320
Pages 130,131

R & R Orchards
951 Houtztown Rd.
Myerstown, PA 17067
(717) 933-8337
Pages 158,159

Binghams Orchard, Inc.
9823 Lincoln Way West
St. Thomas, PA 17252
Pages 128,129,180

Soergel Orchards
2573 Brandt School Rd.
Wexford, PA 15090
(412) 935-1743
Pages 15,134,135,200,201

Shultz Farm Foods
245 Co. Rd. 603
Athens, TN 37303-9604
(615) 745-4723
Page 40

The Apple Barn of Southern
    Vermont Orchards
Carpenter Hill Road
Box 3581
Bennington, VT 05201
(802) 447-7780
Pages 160,161,162

Crow Hill Orchard
R.F.D. 2, Crow Hill
St. Johnsbury, VT 05819
(802) 748-3208
Page 121

Cold Hollow Cider Mill
Route 100, Box 430
Waterbury Center, VT
05677-9704
(802) 244-8771
Pages 92,93,212,213

Waqua Farm Orchard
1058 Rawlings Road
Rawlings, VA 23876
(804) 949-7227
Pages 164,165

Ski-Hi Fruit Farm
E11219 A Ski-Hi Road
Rt. 4
Baraboo, WI 53913
Pages 16,17,24,25,36,37,
136,137,166,167,168,182,183

Bayfield Apple Co.
Route 1, Box 194C
Bayfield, WI 54814
(715) 779-5700
1-800-363-4JAM
Pages 206,207,232,233

Betzold's Orchard
R.R. 1, Box 19
Bayfield, WI 54814-9707
(715) 779-3207
Pages 220,221,222

Hauser's Superior View Farm
Rt. 1, Box 199
Bayfield, WI 54814
Pages 214,215

Arneson Orchard
Rt. l, Box 259A
Blair, WI 54616
Pages 175,181

Fleming Orchards
Rt. 2
Gays Mills, WI 54631
Pages 20,21,138,139

Kickapoo Orchard, Inc.
Rt. 2
Gays Mills, WI 54631
Pages 198,199

Countryside Apple Center
330 56th Ave.
Kenosha, WI 53144
Pages 163,223

Glennie Orchard
18970 W. National Ave.
New Berlin, WI 53146
Pages 169,170,171,242

Recipe Index

Accompaniments

Apple and Cheese Strudel, 79
Apples and Sweet Potato Bake, 82
Apple Cheese Casserole, 83
Apple Cider Sauce, 85
Apple Stuffing, 81
Barbecue Sauce, 85
Candied Apples, 73
Cheese and Apples, 77
Cider Basting for Turkey, 80
Fried Jonathans, 71
Microwave Applesauce, 70
Stuffed Crystallized Apples, 75

Beverages

Hot Spiced Cider, 3
Old-Fashioned Apple Punch, 5

Breads, Loaf

Apple Boston Bread, 37
Apple Bread, Anderson, 28
Apple Bread, Brown, 33
Apple Bread, Shultz, 40
Apple Kuchen, 39
Apple/Nut/Cheese Bread, 31
Apple-Nut Loaf, 35
Apple-Raisin Loaves, 29

Cakes

Apple Cake, Hershberger, 119
Apple Cake, Kriner, 129
Apple Cake, Mickey, 133
Apple Cake, Soergel, 135
Apple Nut Cake, 121
Apple Pie Cake, 113
Apple Pudding Cake, 131
Applesauce Cake, Adae, 117
Applesauce Cake, Fleming, 139
Applesauce Pound Cake, 124

Baked Apple Squares, 121
Best Ladies Aid Apple Cake, 111
Cinnamon-Apple Cake, 137
Cocoa Apple Cake, 115
Emma's Apple Cake, 107
Fresh-Apple Cake, 125
German Apple Cake, 114
Mom's Apple Sauce Cake, 109
Nobby Apple Cake, 123
Old Fashioned Apple Cake, 105
Roman Apple Cake, 127

Coffee Cakes

Apple Coffee Cake, 17
Quick Apple Nut Coffee Cake, 14
Raisin Harvest Coffee Cake, 15
Sour Cream Apple Coffee Cake, 19

Cookies

Amy Quackenbush's Glazed
    Fresh Apple Cookies, 91
Apple Brownies, 97
Apple Butter Bars, 99
Apple Cheddar Scones, 93
Apple Toffee Bars, 101
Caramel Apple Bars, 95
Gas Pedals, 102
Glazed Apple Cookies, 89
"Lean" Brownies, 100

Desserts

Adae's Apple Crisp, 195
All-Time Favorite Apple Crisp, 189
Apple-Berry Shortcake, 230
Apple Bread Pudding, 229
Apple Cranberry Crisp, 197
Apple Cranberry Dessert, 227
Apple Crisp for Microwave, 180
Apple Crisp in a Hurry, 222
Apple Delight, 209
Apple Fritters, 207
Apple Krumbee Crisp, 193
Apple Pudding, 219
Apple Sorbet, 225

Apple Surprise, 217
Apple Tarts, 213
Apple Torte, 221
Autumn Harvest Cheesecake, 205
Bavarian Apple Torte, 211
Cheese Bars, 215
Cider Pudding, 218
Crockpot Applesauce, 189
Hugus' Apple Pizza, 203
Kickapoo Apple Pizza, 198
Krueger's Apple Crisp, 186
Linda's Favorite Apple Crisp, 191
Microwave Apple Crisp, 181
Mincer's Apple Crisp, 185
Mini Apple Pizza, 204
Ochs' Apple Crisp, 194
Orange-Coconut Apple Crisp, 183
Our Favorite Apple Crisp, 190
Ozark Pudding, 216
Quick Apple Dessert, 187
Quick Easy Microwave Apple
    Dessert, 179
Simple Baked Apples, 223
Soergel's Apple Pizza, 201

Jams, Preserves, etc.

Apple Butter, Hugus, 234
Apple Butter, Stephenson, 236
Apple Leather, 238
Bayfield Apple Jam, 233
Drying Apples, 237

Main Dishes

Applesauce Meatloaf, 65
Apple Sausage Roll, 67
Breakfast Apples, 63
Chicken Caprice, 64

Muffins

A.B.C. Muffins, 27
Apple Muffins, 25
Apple Streusel Muffins, 21
Fresh Apple Muffins, 23

Pancakes

Apple Puff Pancake, 12
Gene's Oven Pancakes, 10

Pies and Pastry

Apfelkuchen, 174
Apple Cider Pie, 147
Apple Pastry, 176
Apple Pastry Bars, 171
Apple Pie, 144
Apple Pie A'Plenty, 153
Apple Pie in a Bag, 159
Apple Pie in Squares, 155
Apple Rosettes, 168
Apple Squares, 175
Bumbleberry Pie, 161
Diehl's Apple Pie, 151
Easy Apple Pie, 165
French Apple Pie, 149
Glennie Orchard Dutch Apple
    Pie, 170
Krueger's Apple Dumplings, 172
No Sugar Apple Pie, 162
Old World Open Face Apple
    Pie, 163
Prairie Spy Pastry, 145
Schweizer's Apple Dumplings, 173
Surprise Apple Twists, 167
Topsy Turvy Apple Pie, 157

Salads

A.B.C. Salad, 45
Apple Compote, 43
Apple Pickers' Favorite Apple
    Salad, 53
Apple Salad, 51
Buckingham's Waldorf Slaw, 59
Double Apple Salad, 49
Fruit and Rice Salad, 47
Ochs' Waldorf Salad, 57
Quick Applesauce Salad, 44
Waldorf Salad, 55

Special Treats

Apple Spread, 240
Apple Dip, 242
Fruit Dip, 241

Toppings for Cakes

Caramel/Coconut Frosting, 105
Caramel Frosting, 139
Caramel Topping, 140
Cream Cheese Frosting, 140
Lemon Sauce, 140
Rum Butter Sauce, 113
Sauce, 119
Topping, 127

LEONA NOVY JACKSON

A love of the orchard and all things "apple" have prompted Lee Jackson to write her second cookbook about apples. This time she wanted to focus on the apple growers and what they do with apples when they use this fruit for their family and guests. She wanted to tour their orchards and taste their fruit. This is what you can do as you "travel" throughout the country sampling the fruit from over 65 of America's orchards and preparing apple dishes just the way growers and those in the apple and food industry fix them. If you have a bushel of apples or only a few, you will find recipes that will entice you into trying "just one more new way" with apples.

Leona Novy Jackson first became interested in apples when she was growing up and helping in the apple orchard on her family's farm in Wisconsin. Later, as a high school family and consumer science teacher (formerly home economics) she brought to the classroom a study of the nutritional value of apples and helped students learn how to include them in their diets in many different ways.

Lee received a B.S. degree in home economics education from the University of Wisconsin-Stout, Menomonie, Wisconsin, and an M.S. in education from Northwest Missouri State University, Maryville, Missouri. After having taught in schools in Wisconsin and over 20 years at Maryville R-II High School, Maryville, Missouri, Lee now enjoys writing about food, children and parenting, family, careers, and other themes related to the home. She and her husband, Peter, live in Missouri and at their cabin in northern Minnesota, where she continues to nurture her interest in trees, including apple trees and their fruit.